Helion & Company Limited
Unit 8 Amherst Business Centre
Budbrooke Road
Warwick
CV34 5WE
England
Tel. 01926 499 619
Email: info@helion.co.uk
Website: www.helion.co.uk
Twitter: @helionbooks
Visit our blog http://blog.helion.co.uk/

Designed & typeset by Farr out Publications, Wokingham, Berkshire
Cover design by Paul Hewitt, Battlefield Design (www.battlefield-design.co.uk)

ISBN 978-1-804513-62-0

British Library Cataloguing-in-Publication Data
A catalogue record for this book is available from the British Library

We always welcome receiving book proposals from prospective authors.

CONTENTS

Note: In order to simplify the use of this book, all names, locations and geographic designations are as provided in *The Times World Atlas*, or other traditionally accepted major sources of reference, as of the time of described events. Correspondingly, the term 'Congo' designates the area of the former Belgian colony of the Congo Free State, granted independence as the Democratic Republic of the Congo in June 1960 and in use until 1971 when the country was renamed Republic of Zaire, which, in turn, reverted to Democratic Republic of the Congo in 1997, and which remains in use today. As such, Congo is not to be mistaken for the former French colony of Middle Congo (Moyen Congo), officially named the Republic of the Congo on its independence in August 1960, also known as Congo-Brazzaville.

Glossary

Agric Alert	a system that connected famers together which would be triggered when an attack took place to summon help
AGL	above ground level
B.S.A.P.	British South Africa Police
Casevac	casualty evacuation, generally a military term indicating someone with s serious injury that requires immediate medical care
Contact	combat
CT	communist terrorist, also terrorist or terr or gook
DCA	Directorate of Civil Aviation
FAF	Forward Airfield
G-car	Alouette III SA316B helicopter with a crew of two and four fully equipped troops, sometimes armed
JOC	Joint Operational Command
K-car	Alouette III SA316B helicopter with a crew of two and the Fire Force Commander. Armed with twin mounted Browning .303 machine guns and later 20mm cannon
Kopje	a small rocky hill
Landtail	ground based and transported element of a Fire Force formation
Magandanga	terrorists, Shona language
Mujiba	mostly young male nationalist supporters who acted as messengers and gathered information. *Mujiba* in Shona means 'in the field' the eyes and ears of the insurgents
Masodja	RAR soldier or troops
O.P.	Observation Post
ORAF	Old Rhodesian Air Force
The Outpost Magazine	the official magazine of the British South Africa Police
PATU	Police Anti-Terrorist Unit
PGHQ	Police General Headquarters
PRAW	Police Reserve Air Wing
PRO	Police Reserve Observer
PRP	Police Reserve Pilot
RAR	Rhodesian African Rifles Regiment
RhAF	Rhodesian Air Force
RRAF	Royal Rhodesian Air Force up until UDI
RSF	Rhodesian Security Forces
Salisbury	the capital of Rhodesia now Harare Zimbabwe
SALOPS	Salisbury Operations
SFA	Special Forces Auxiliary
Stick	usually a group of four to six police or army patrol
Troopie	Rhodesian soldier
TTL	Tribal Trust Land
ZANLA	Zimbabwe African National Liberation Army

Preface

The father of history, Herodotus, wrote that his 'own responsibility … is simply to record whatever I may have been told by my sources.' Following this principle certain terms and names used in the narrative are of the time. It is distracting to see both old and new place names in the text and as the first-hand accounts will always refer to names that existed at the time, these have been retained. In a similar manner the terminology used with reference to the groups that opposed the Rhodesian government largely remain as they were used at the time. The use of these is for historical and contextual reasons and is not, in any way, political. The main text is followed by direct submissions from crew members as they recall their experiences and have been retained largely unedited as they form an important record of the history of this time, albeit some terms then in use are not common today.

I am indebted to Bill Linfield, who served for a time as the commander of the unit, for his invaluable support to this project. He was the inspiration for the structure of the work and has contributed so much in the way of content, corrections and answering a myriad of follow up questions. Anthony Trethowan, Brian van Buuren, Bob Fernandes, John Steed, Gerry Cleveland, John Munro, Bob Needham, Peter Marchussen, Tony Mann, Mike Norton, John Tayler, Doug Towler, and Richard Wood, all provided me with their stories or allowed me to quote from their books. While Orlie Anderson facilitated phone calls with her mother Shelagh, who sadly passed away within a few weeks of our last call. Dave and Julian Scales spent time on the phone telling me about their father Peter and Andrew Watson wrote about his father's Beechcraft Bonanza. Mimi Cawood related her experiences as a radio operator stationed at Beit Bridge and introduced me to Don Price who filled in the events that happened on the southern border. Andrew Tefler, ex RAR was always available to provide context and detail relevant to this unit. Late in the day I contacted Rod Bater, who kindly took the time to fill in some important detail. Hugh Bomford of The Lion & Tusk – Museum of the Rhodesian Services Association in Mount Maunganui www.thelionandtusk.org, put the word out to members and Sue Onslow allowed me to reference her work with Rhodesian ex-servicemen.

Thank you to all those who provided their photographs and access to the articles referenced. Particularly Alan Murray's family and friends and especially Keith Holshausen who rescued several of *The Outpost* images that had been thrown away. To Eduard Pietersen who sadly passed away in early 2022 for his help and comments. Special thanks to Robin Norton who had the foresight to record Rhodesian aviation history on film. It is a privilege to have his permission to use some of his images that have added a valuable element to this work. Every effort has been made to establish and acknowledge ownership of the images provided.

There will no doubt be errors and questions, but this kind of work is not an exact science. It subject to the passing of time, lack of original documents and my understanding of what I am told.

Thank you to Tanya De Leersnyder for her support at all levels throughout this two year project.

Guy Ellis
Gloucestershire 2022

1
Towards the end

It was clear in the documents captured from ZANLA insurgents, that taking the capital city, Salisbury, was an important strategic goal. The first blow was struck when an eight-man force attacked a fuel depot in the city's Southerton area. The rockets fired on 11 December 1978 set fire to the huge storage tanks, destroying 25 million gallons of precious fuel.

SALOPS – Salisbury Operations

ZANLA commanders focused on moving their forces from Mozambique into Rhodesia and by early 1979, the TTLs to the north and east of Salisbury were 'liberated' areas, where only the small towns were held by the RSF. Patrols were conducted in these areas, but any gains were not held for long. Manpower was in short supply, as white emigration soared, and the economy suffered from continual military call-ups of the workforce. To bolster the RSF the Transitional Government, formed on 3 March 1978 to pave the way to majority rule, had created Security Force Auxiliaries (SFA). This force was comprised of the armed wings of the new partners in the Government, former insurgents, and the general population in the townships. The SFA, which eventually numbered 10,000, were sent into the TTLs to counter ZANLA politically and militarily.

Chief Inspector M. J. (Fred) Pringle, in late 1978, created a new Police Reserve Air Wing (PRAW) flight, Salisbury Operations (SALOPS), which provided crews to support ground forces in the defence of the city. Selected younger PRAW crews were drafted into the SALOPS wing, the only dedicated combat-only wing in PRAW. This group no longer served at FAFs or provided courier or casevac flights. The aircraft were armed with Browning machine guns, or MAGs, and at times anti-personnel bombs.

While on operations a PRAW pilot found the PATU patrol he was working with was struggling to remember which 'Copper' number to use. He instructed the PATU radio operator to call him 'Snoopy'. Communications worked after that and the SALOPS flight adopted this term as their call sign. The famous cartoon character Snoopy was drafted in to support the SALOPS Flight. (Photo by Wayne Kennerley)

Pilots used whichever aircraft was available of the four allocated to the unit. There was always one aircraft on active duty and one on standby, which did not leave much leeway when maintenance or repairs from ground fire damage were being carried out on one of the aircraft.

'ZS-ZGZ was one of several Cessna 206 aircraft (both U206 and P206 variants),' Tony Mann, Copper 282 recorded, 'allocated to the SALOPS Recce Flight of the Rhodesian armed forces for Forward Air Control (FAC) and reconnaissance purposes and served as such until the conclusion of hostilities during March 1980.'[1]

Virtually outside the company hangar is Piper PA-28 Cherokee 180C VP-WAG owned by Techair. This company's aircraft were often used for PRAW flights pilots as they were based near to the capital. (Robin D. W. Norton)

SALOPS STAND-BY ROSTER : 21/4 - 29/6/79

During this period, the Flight will revert to one aircraft and crew on daily stand-by between 0800 and 1800 hours daily unless otherwise advised. The Reserve crews and aircraft must be available at two hours notice, and SALOPS are to be advised of telephone number if other than home or work. Duty-swapping amongst crews is perfectly acceptable, but SALOPS and Flight Commander must be advised.

DATE		STAND-BY CREWS	RESERVES
APRIL	21 - 27	CLEVELAND & CHAPPE	HARVEY & SEWARD
APR/MAY	28/4-4/5	BROWN & OLDBURY	PRINGLE & JOHNSON
MAY	5/5-11/5	PRINGLE & JOHNSON	MURRAY & PEINKE
MAY	12/5-18/5	MURRAY & PEINKE	CLEVELAND & CHAPPE
MAY	19/5-25/5	CLEVELAND & CHAPPE	BROWN & OLDBURY
MAY/JN	26/5-1/6	BROWN & OLDBURY	PRINGLE & JOHNSON
JUNE	2/6-8/6	PRINGLE & JOHNSON	HARVEY & SEWARD
JUNE	9/6-15/6	HARVEY & SEWARD	MURRAY & PEINKE
JUNE	16/6-22/6	MURRAY & PEINKE	CLEVELAND & CHAPPE
JUNE	23/6-29/6	CLEVELAND & CHAPPE	BROWN & OLDBURY

Further Roster will be published in due course.

Observer Chandler will be available for casual replacement duties for the time being until initial acceptance test for Pilot rating has been passed.

Pilot Anderson and Observer Thorogood are available for casual replacement duties as and when required, but as far as possible adequate notice must be given please.

*** FLIGHT MEETINGS will be held on the 11th MAY and 8th JUNE at 6.pm. Please Diarise and attend. Venue is the small lounge in the Copperpot.

This notice shows that one crew are to be standby between 0800 to 1800 daily. The reserve crews were ordered to be available at two hours' notice. Swapping between crews was allowed if SALOPS and the Flight Commander were advised. (Photo by Alan Murray)

- 5 -

SALOPS RECCE FLIGHT

		Operational C/S
280	BROWN R.C. 16827P	ALPHA ZERO
281	CLEVELAND G.M. 9191W	ALPHA ONE
282	MANN A.T. 31739Y	ALPHA TWO
283	ANDERSON D.O. 27323X	ALPHA THREE
284	PRINGLE I.N. 20159L	ALPHA FOUR
285		ALPHA FIVE
286	SIMPSON P. 31819K	ALPHA SIX
287	ADDISON A.C. 22509C	ALPHA SEVEN
288		ALPHA EIGHT
289		ALPHA NINE
290	ROBERTS A.J.H. 30118L	
291	ELLIOT, D.G. 34054P	
292	PARISH G.P.J. 24065G	
293		
294		
295		
296		
297		
298		
299		

Doug Elliot, G. P. J. Parish and A. J. H. Roberts were members of the Salisbury Gliding Club and were used by SALOPS HQ on a casual and infrequent basis, and were assigned specific reconnaissance duties flying the Gliding Club's Super Cub and Auster 5 VP YJX. As noted, these pilots did not have operational call signs and unlike the other aircraft in the Flight, the aircraft were not armed. (Photo by Tony Mann)

Inspector Graham McCleland 8577 and his wife 208 Lois McCleland in 1979. Notice the PRAW roster board behind Lois's shoulder showing Tony Mann and Dave Moss on duty and on standby George Harvey and Richard Seward. (*The Outpost Magazine*)

Tony Mann, left and Ian Pringle with VP-WFO following an intensive and successful operation during which there were several bullet strikes to the port wing and fuselage of the aircraft. The gunner struggled with wind noise from the open doorway and the standard military headset was inadequate. The air force provided the helmets held by the crew, which had superior headsets that improved communications between the crew and with ground forces. (Photo by Tony Mann)

He went on to note that 'the endurance with the 206, at the specified power settings, was typically 5 hours, which effectively meant that we could operate from dawn to dusk (which did indeed happen on occasions), with only one stop for refuelling, rearmament and whatever refreshment could be found.

'My personal logbook reflects activities with ZS-ZGZ during January 1980 and is typical of the required duties. The gunnery practice conducted on 27 January would have simply been the alignment and harmonisation of the weapon prior to the forthcoming operations while the balance of the entries reflects either 'Ground Air Control'

At one time owned by PRP Rupert Hildebrand, Cessna 180 VP-WAV was photographed in February 1971 about to take off from Excelsior airstrip close to Salisbury Airport during flight test from Fields Aircraft Services, conducted by ex-air force pilot Mike Saunders. (Robin D. W. Norton)

Cessna 206 Super Skylane, probably VP-WCK is seen over water on a grey day. Tony Mann wrote that this aircraft was one of the few with the full anti-Strela modification of both matte grey finish and the shrouded exhausts. The aircraft saw infrequent use with SALOPS, although he did recall several flights as the gunner. (Photo by Tony Mann)

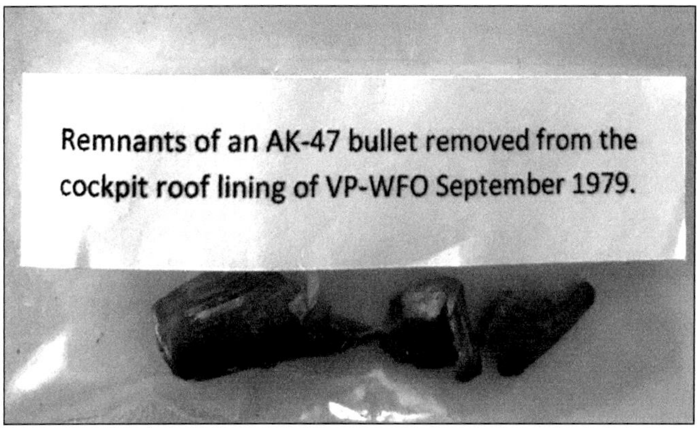

For SALOPS operations, VP-WFO was the aircraft of choice as it was the only Cessna 206 in the unit with the gun on the left. Having the gunner and the pilot on the same side of the aircraft was more effective. During a left-hand orbit over a target, 'Foxtrot Oscar' again took ground fire. An AK47 round entered the aircraft through the undercarriage box, hit the edge of the bulletproof seat on which Tony Mann was sitting, which deflected it into the roof lining. Tony, realising it had not exited through the upper surfaces managed to retrieve the remains from within the headlining. (Photo by Tony Mann)

(i.e. Forward Air Control) or reconnaissance duties.'

An experienced pilot, Tony Mann joined SALOPS as a pilot with Ian Pringle. Within a short time of joining, he broke his ankle in a skydiving accident. His leg in plaster did not deter SALOPS command. He was trained as an observer/gunner and served as Ian's crewman until his injury healed. When he regained his wings and was allocated his own gunner, Dave Moss, and the two of them remained together until SALOPS was dissolved.

Attacks on farms and installations and further intelligence spurred the Rhodesian Government to gather a powerful force together, headquartered at the Enterprise Sports Club. An element of this force was two PRAW aircraft from Charles Prince Airfield, with one positioned daily at Frascati Farm, in the north of the operational area.

Operation Enterprise, which Mike Norton, Special Branch Office SALOPS, subtitles as the Battle for Salisbury, ran from the 6 to 20 April 1979. In his article on the operation, Mike Norton wrote that the PRAW, 'aircraft were used in support of ground call signs and proved very effective in, if nothing else, slowing insurgent groups down, and allowing pursuing troops to catch up. They did achieve some kills with their air gunnery and provided much-needed air support when helicopters were unavailable.'[2]

From the PRAW perspective, Tony Mann said that,

> Although we were required to work with any ground forces that needed our assistance, most of our operations were conducted together with motorcyclists from various PATU units. This proved to be an extremely efficient manner of follow-up as the motorcycles (typically 250cc trail bikes with very effective silencing) could obviously cover the necessary distances far quicker than any infantry. Constant communication was maintained between the motorcyclists and the aircraft that would be orbiting overhead and observing any indications of enemy activity.[3]

The capture of a ZANLA platoon commander revealed that what was known as the Salisbury detachment had been ordered to move back to regroup and resupply. The battle had been won but the war

12th December 1979

B.S.A.P.
Salops
P.O. Box 8028
CAUSEWAY
Salisbury

ATTENTION: D. Pretorius

REPORT ON INCIDENT INVOLVING AIRCRAFT VPW CP - 24TH JULY 1979

On the morning of the 24th July 1979 the undersigned and P/R Pilot I. Pringle were called upon to assist ground forces in a follow-up operation in the southern Chikwakwa T.T.L. (approximate locstat UR 445379).

Ground forces consisted of six motor cyclists from 2̶57 and after locating these call signs we were requested to orbit ahead of their intended sweep to observe any movement and also drown out the noise of their approach.

Approximately thirty minutes after commencing the exercise we observed a single A.M.A. dressed in heavy clothing leaving the cover of a kopje and proceeding towards a kraal line. Due to the suspect's erratic activities we requested that the ground forces intercept and interrogate. When the ground forces approached within 200 metres of the suspect, they were subjected to small arms fire and in the ensuing contact the suspect removed his overcoat and proceeded to run for the cover of a rocky outcrop and river line between 1½ and 2 kilometres distant, whilst at the same time returning fire.

On initiating the contact, the suspect was subject to fire by both ourselves and ground forces and within a few minutes we came under heavy ground small arms fire and received one hit through the port elevator of the aircraft. The number of C.T.'s involved in this firing is unknown nor was their whereabouts established by ourselves.

The suspect eventually managed to take refuge in the river line and bordering feature and in the ensuing sweep operation was finally killed and one A.K. rifle and webbing recovered.

Damage to the aircraft was of a superficial nature with the bullet entering the tail plane at a 45° angle from the rear but causing no structural damage and necessitating only repair to the upper and lower elevator skins. Skyworks invoice in respect of this damage is attached herewith.

A.T. MANN
31739Y

This report covers a flight on 24 July 1979 manned by Tony Mann and PRP Ian Pringle and flying a Cessna 182A Skylane VP-WCP. While in support of motorbike mounted ground forces they fired on an armed suspect and, in turn, came under heavy small arms, which resulted in non-structural gunfire damage to the tailplane. (Photo by Tony Mann)

continued. The Chikakwa, Msana, and Chinamora TTLs were all held by the RSF, supported by the SFA, enterprise farmers and PATU.

A notable incident in which the SALOPS wing played an important role was the follow-up operation to find Mrs Yvonne Mulligan, who had been abducted from a farm on the afternoon of 14 July 1979. Tracks showed that she had been moved into an area heavily populated that was flat, sandy, and offered little natural cover. Two PRAW aircraft were sent to cover the area and prevent any further movement of the captive. Follow-up forces found themselves in a fully liberated area and were regularly engaging with small groups of insurgents. PRAW provided armed cover until darkness fell.

While attacking insurgents in a kraal a Fire Force K-car was hit. Mike Norton recorded that 'orbiting above was PRAW Copper 47, pilot Hamish Harvey, who broke into the radio net to tell K2 that they were on fire in the K2 engine area.' The Alouette sustained further strikes before the pilot managed to put it down. All the crew were rescued by a G-car. The insurgents managed to move their abductee to Mozambique; she was returned to Rhodesia in December 1979.

Flying hours increased from 383 in 1961 to 22,000 in 1977, flown by 180 pilots and observers. In 1978 the hours increased to 25,000 and again increased to an unknown number in 1979.The following table was provided by the B.S.A.P. on 7 August 1979.

Year	PRAW aircraft in service	Number aircraft hit by gunfire during contact
1974	40	3
1975	50	0
1976	80	1
1977	90	5
1978	102	7
1979 to July	120	32

Two aircraft were destroyed on farm airstrips by rockets and small arms fire. There were only two casualties, with an observer/gunner killed in June 1979, and a pilot sustained serious chest injuries in November 1978.

The B.S.A.P.

A Royal Charter of 1889 authorised the formation of the British South Africa Company constituted to promote colonial expansion and benefit from the expected mineral wealth of the region.

To protect the Pioneer Column, as it entered what was to become Rhodesia, a mounted paramilitary unit was formed and named the British South Africa Company Police. In 1896, the word Company

Beechcraft Bonanza VP-YGZ was one of the first used by the Unit. At the time not owned or flown by a PRAW member it seen here on a recovery trailer after it suffered engine failure shortly after take off from Mount Hamden and force landed in a small quarry adjacent to the airport. Two of the recovery crew, Murra and Michek are talking to someone off camera. (Robin D. W. Norton)

B.S.A.P. Reserve Air Wing members who attended the Flight Commanders Conference on 19 September 1979.
Back row, left to right: Chief Inspector Fred Pringle, PRP P. C. Rawson (Standards Flight), PRP G. J. W. Harvey (Deputy Unit Commander and Flight Commander SALOPS Flight), PRP R. L. Anderson (PGHQ Flight), PRP B. A. Van Buuren (Manicaland Flight), PRP M. H. Garde (Matabeleland Flight), PRP R. E. Style (Victoria flight), Inspector R. G. Bye.
Seated, left to right: PRP V A D Browne (Midlands Flight), PRP J L Manning (Lomagundi Flight), PRP P. P. Palmer (Deputy Director of Civil Aviation), Assistant Commissioner B. L. Nightingale (Senior Staff Officer Police Reserve), PRP J. F. Plant (Unit Commander), PRP W. J. Ludgater (Mazoe Flight), PRP H. V. Chisnall (Marandellas Flight), PRO G. D. Pearce (Unit Aviation Engineer). (Wayne Kennerley Collection)

Originally the British South Africa Company wanted the Regimental Badge of the B.S.A. Police to be an image of one of their troopers on a horse, but this idea appears to have been very quickly vetoed by the Colonial Office or the Royal Mint. The final design is a modification of the obverse of the British South Africa Company Medal.
The insignia of the B.S.A.P.; as described in British Battles and Medals as: 'A charging lion with a spear (Assegai) sticking in its chest. In the background is a mimosa bush, and in the foreground are a native shield and spears.' The symbolism is showing the lion (Great Britain) even though it has been injured overcoming the aggressors and defeating them, hence the lion on top of discarded shields and assegai. The motto reads *Pro Rege, Pro Lege, Pro Partria* (For King, For Law, For Country). It was in use until 1980. (Image Universal Uniform UK, Research Paul Brewster)[4]

Mount Hampden in the early 1970s where it would appear this Cherokee had received some attention. VP-YVH, a Piper PA-28-160 Cherokee was listed on BASP Nominal Roll of Aircraft in use with the wing as at 1 March 1974. The Ground crew would refuel and swing the props of the Mashonaland Flying Clubs Cubs and Tiger Moths. (Robin D. W. Norton)

was dropped, taking on a civilian policing role, and in 1909 it came under Imperial Government control.

The paramilitary influences remained throughout its existence. Members were trained as policemen and soldiers, serving in both World Wars. During the Rhodesian bush war, the B.S.A.P., in its military and civilian roles was initially the senior arm of the Government. As the conflict escalated into a full war, the army assumed this role.

Specialised military units were created. The Police Anti-Terrorist Unit (PATU) was actively engaged in combat against the insurgents, a Support Unit, which was a police field force, a Civilian Tracking Unit, an Urban Emergency Unit, a Police Reserve Air Wing (PRAW), a Marine Division, and from 1973 national service conscripts could serve in the police.

The BSAP was disbanded on 1 August 1980 and replaced by the Zimbabwe Republic Police.

2
The End Game

As recorded in Tony Mann's logbook, all SALOPS activities were formally, and unceremoniously, terminated on 10 March 1980 with orders being given for the immediate destruction of all records pertaining to the unit. The final SALOPS flight of any nature was flown by Tony on 12 March 1980 utilising ZS-ZGZ to retrieve PRAW records for destruction from New Sarum Air Force base at Salisbury Airport.

The last two flights for Alan Abrey were memorable. As he was twin rated and licensed to fly a ZS registered aircraft he was required to fly Joshua Nkomo to Thornhill and Kumalo on 26 March 1980 in a Techair Aztec ZS-EIG. His last PRAW flight took place on 18 April 1980, when he flew two ministers from the new Mugabe Government along with an army and police officer from the former Rhodesian forces to Kotwa airfield beyond Mtoko for the 'independence celebrations'. Alan wrote that on landing:

> [they] were met by 12 ZANLA troops who were to guard my plane while others drove us to an Assembly point three miles away where apparently 3,500 ZANLA troops under the command of 'Edward' were assembled. We were met at the entrance by Edward and then escorted under close guard to a parade ground of sorts and were seated on a slightly elevated dais under poles and grass. Every single man was armed but very few had any sort of uniform. We were served tea and thick sandwiches by woman ZANLA members in uniform while a Chinese Bayonet Drill was performed by about 100 troops.[1]

The ministers and the commander praised their forces for their victory and read out many congratulatory messages from Communist and OAU countries.

The new state of Zimbabwe came into existence on 18 April 1980. The Police Reserve Air Wing's name was changed to Police Air Wing (PAW), and the pilots became Police Pilots. They reverted to civilian

British Airways Flight BA051 operated by a Boeing 747 G-BDXE, on 10 January 1980 was the first direct London to Salisbury service since sanctions were imposed in 1965. Tony Mann wrote:

> … there was some concern that there may be an attempt to disrupt the arrival from a propaganda perspective. We were therefore instructed to patrol the airport approach for a period prior to the arrival of BA051 to ensure it was clear of any suspicious activity. Once the aircraft was safely established on final approach, we elected to land ahead (to avoid any wake turbulence) and then immediately parked on one of the taxiways to observe its safe arrival. I was fortunately allowed to bring a camera with me on this occasion and was able to capture the rather unique image.[2] (Photo by Tony Mann)

policing, and the demand for PRAW's service dropped to 20 percent of that over the previous five years. The unit still covered a lot of ground. They flew in food to drought-ravaged areas, continued with their courier services and casevac flights. Using their recce experience they formed an anti-poaching unit in conjunction with wildlife organisations.

From 1980 PRAW pilots were known as Police Pilots with the Police Air Wing (PAW), this group were photographed after they had taken part in a fly past during the Air Tattoo in Harare on 16 October 1995. The main attraction of the day was the display by the RAF Red Arrows
Front row, left to right: Observer Elijah Chirimuuta Pilots van Vuuren, Steed, Linfield, Maxwell
Middle row, left to right: Observer Rowley, Pilots Carson, Taylor, Bater, Mitch Rodgers, du Preez
Back row, left to right: Unknown. (Photo by John Steed)

One of these was 'Operation Stronghold', which was set up to combat the devastating poaching of black rhino in the Zambezi Valley. Mark Brightman reported, on the ORAFs site[3] that during this campaign in the mid-1980s PAW offered their assistance. In 1986 he was ranger based at Nyamoumba, at the downstream mouth of the Kariba Gorge. One of PAW's major roles was to carry out routine aerial surveys to detect carcasses, poachers' camps, and assessing both perennial and annual water supplies. They would monitor any suspicious Zambian vehicle and boat activity along the Zambezi River. The disused, but still operational Sharu airstrip some 9km east of the station itself, was used.

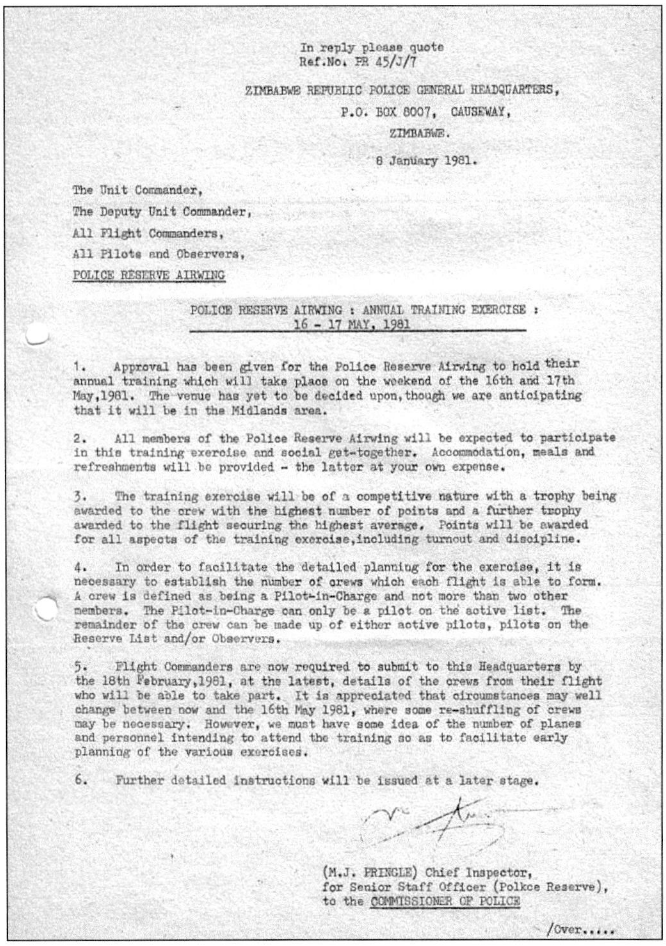

In reply please quote
Ref.No. PR 45/J/7

ZIMBABWE REPUBLIC POLICE GENERAL HEADQUARTERS,
P.O. BOX 8007, CAUSEWAY,
ZIMBABWE.

8 January 1981.

The Unit Commander,
The Deputy Unit Commander,
All Flight Commanders,
All Pilots and Observers,
POLICE RESERVE AIRWING

POLICE RESERVE AIRWING : ANNUAL TRAINING EXERCISE :
16 - 17 MAY, 1981

1. Approval has been given for the Police Reserve Airwing to hold their annual training which will take place on the weekend of the 16th and 17th May,1981. The venue has yet to be decided upon, though we are anticipating that it will be in the Midlands area.

2. All members of the Police Reserve Airwing will be expected to participate in this training exercise and social get-together. Accommodation, meals and refreshments will be provided - the latter at your own expense.

3. The training exercise will be of a competitive nature with a trophy being awarded to the crew with the highest number of points and a further trophy awarded to the flight securing the highest average. Points will be awarded for all aspects of the training exercise, including turnout and discipline.

4. In order to facilitate the detailed planning for the exercise, it is necessary to establish the number of crews which each flight is able to form. A crew is defined as being a Pilot-in-Charge and not more than two other members. The Pilot-in-Charge can only be a pilot on the active list. The remainder of the crew can be made up of either active pilots, pilots on the Reserve List and/or Observers.

5. Flight Commanders are now required to submit to this Headquarters by the 18th February,1981, at the latest, details of the crews from their flight who will be able to take part. It is appreciated that circumstances may well change between now and the 16th May 1981, where some re-shuffling of crews may be necessary. However, we must have some idea of the number of planes and personnel intending to attend the training so as to facilitate early planning of the various exercises.

6. Further detailed instructions will be issued at a later stage.

(M.J. PRINGLE) Chief Inspector,
for Senior Staff Officer (Polkce Reserve),
to the COMMISSIONER OF POLICE

/Over.....

After the 1980 elections, PRAW was known as the Police Air Wing (PAW), and they were used in the civilian policing role. Things continued in very much the same way, even training days such as this held over two days in May 1981 was conducted on the same basis as those that had gone before. (Photo by Dave Moss, Copper 281)

Peter Thorne, Copper 180, service number 24827K, displaying ribbons of the Zimbabwe Independence Medal, Rhodesia General Service Medal, and Medal for Territorial or Reserve Service. The medal to commemorate the independence of Zimbabwe was suggested by Lord Christopher Soames, the head of the Commonwealth Monitoring Force (CMF). The CMF oversaw the first inclusive election and the birth of Zimbabwe. (Photo by Bill Linfield)

John Plant, the PRAW commander, briefs the PRAW crews taking part in an exercise in 1981. To his right is Hamish Harvey and behind him is Richard Seaward who flew as Hamish's observer. (Photo by Gerry Cleveland)

Seen at Bulawayo Main in the late 1990s is Roger Fenner, once Copper 75 of the Matabeleland flight, with Piper Cherokee Arrow Z-WGZ. A memorable flight in the then VP-WGZ was a six-hour patrol over the Kezi area at almost impossible power settings to conserve fuel to be able to remain on station. (Photo by Nic Fenner)

On 30 August 1986, a low-level routine flight with pilot, a Mr Wilcox, and observer in Z–WOT was carried out in the Nyakasanga River area. It was discovered later that the parallel transect flights, following the river valleys had flushed out a poaching gang who, under the impression the aircraft had seen them, returned to Zambia.

The PAW flights continued for the remainder of that year, and when this ended, a WWF funded Jet Ranger helicopter boosted operational capacity enormously. The Zimbabwe Air Force also aided with an Alouette III, and later an AB 205 'Cheetah' when funding to continue with the Jet Ranger became an issue. Mark wrote that 'sadly, not a single rhino remains there today. But we tried our best, with what little resources and funding we could muster.'[4]

There were monthly training sessions and with observer Bill Perkins, Brian van Buuren was called out a few times to search for missing or abducted people. The last major event for the Manicaland Flight was during the 1991/92 drought where 12 aircraft were employed on game counts in the Gonarezhou National Park.

After the ceasefire, a nighttime casevac was Wally Barton's final PAW flight. In the *The Outpost* magazine he wrote that he was called out:

> … to collect two people who were very ill. The airfield was unlit, so I requested a vehicle be parked at each end of the runway

Kirsty Chatham wrote that in later years Jimmy Aitken flew a Piper Comanche and then a Meyers Aero commander 200D, here seen registered as Z-WMD. Neither of these aircraft was used for PRAW duties, but their forced sale following the loss of the farm during Government sponsored farm invasions represent a reason why PAW ceased to operate from the 2000s. (Photo by Jimmy Aitken)

Police Reserve Air Wing's Mazoe Flight, being briefed by Chief Superintendant Trevor Wilson are PR(0) Geoff Gibson, Inspector Joe Surkont, Flight Commander Bill Ludgater, Chief Superintendant Trevor Wilson, PRP Ronnie Pascoe, PR(0) Bruce Reed, PR(0) Dougie Lyon, PRP Micky Anthony, PRP Mike Dawson and PRP Mike Alford. (The Outpost Magazine)

Flown by Bill Ludgater, Copper 03, of the Mazoe Flight this Cessna 180F VP-YTV was at the Centenary Air Show in May 1972. Notable is the BSAP insignia on the vertical stabiliser. (Robin Norton)

> with the headlights pointing across the runway. They parked the vehicles with their lights shining down the runway. I had no radio coms with the ground so had to make the best of it. Then to add insult to injury someone in the camp started firing at me, but the mission was successful.[5]

Following his father's example, Julian Scales had joined PRAW and was called to assist with relief work after Cyclone Leon-Eline devastated large areas of Zimbabwe in February 2000. Battling high winds, they set out to find people isolated by the floodwaters, drop food and direct rescues. This was probably the last time that Police fixed wing aircraft were used.

PAW fell under the Transport Ministry, which found that it did not have the funds to maintain the unit. Without the means to compensate the pilots who in turn could maintain their aircraft, the Wing could not continue. Later in 2000, Government policies forcibly removed commercial farmers from the land. These stalwarts of PAW were left with no means to keep their aircraft. The Wing, no longer viable, ceased to exist in 2002.

3

Preface

Several PRAW members wrote about their experiences and publishing them as written serves as a record of the time in the voices of the men who flew in such a big way.

Wally Barton: Copper 4[1]

Flying has always been in my blood... probably nurtured by the stories my father often told of his time in the RFC and RAF during the 1914–1918 war. He flew SE5As, and as a fighter pilot achieved considerable success, while fighting in France.

On leaving school at the end of 1941, two of my friends and I set out for Roberts Heights to join the South African Air Force. After a prolonged spell of training, due to many RAF personnel being sent to South Africa to be trained as aircrew, two of us were posted to the UK on secondment to the RAF along with 73 other SAAF pilots. After further advanced training, I was posted to No 515 Squadron where I flew Mosquitos. We carried out low-level intruder raids over Germany.

From 1946 to 1963, I did no flying. In 1963, several farmers in the Centenary East area arranged for a flying instructor from Techair to fly out to Panorama airstrip once a week to give flying lessons. I had to do a five-hour refresher course to qualify as a private pilot. In 1965, I was able to import a Cessna 182 direct from America.

I immediately applied for a transfer from the Police Reserve to PRAW. When this was granted, I became a member of the Mazoe Valley flight commanded by Bill Ludgater. Our tasks at this time were many and varied and included the collection and delivery of spare parts. We flew hundreds of courier flights. I had as passengers all ranks from generals to prisoners and flew into the most remote and varied airstrips some barely qualifying as landing grounds. These strips were situated all over Rhodesia, so we gained a good knowledge of the country and of bad weather flying. Supply drops were a common task and generally involved some interesting flying while making drops in the Zambezi escarpment. Observers who flew with me were Innes Bell, Hammy Dax, Noel (Bundu) Waller,

ON THE COVER

The March 1969 edition of the police magazine showed Cessna 172C VP-YUG, probably piloted by owner Bill MacDonald, Copper 12, and crewed by observer Dickie Boltt, on a sortie over the Zambezi Valley, where in December 1968 they had played an important role in the rescue of a soldier lost in the featureless and unforgiving bushland. (*The Outpost Magazine*)

Mr H F 'Hammy' Dax, a farmer from Centenary, at the controls of his Piper Comanche VP-YYL, was the 'poster boy' for the October 1975 Outpost Magazine. (*The Outpost Magazine*)

The picture of a PRAW crew, observer Mike Browning left and pilot Don Howard, as they prepared for a flight over Manicaland, was the front cover of The Outpost edition of 4 April 1975. (*The Outpost Magazine*)

The cover caption of *The Outpost Magazine* for October 1977 was 'The B.S.A. Police has its first operational woman pilot in the trim figure of Shelagh Anderson, otherwise known as "Copper 165". Shelagh also fills in her non-flying hours as PGHQ Flight Tasking Officer.' (*The Outpost Magazine*)

Wally Barton of the Mazoe Flight owned and flew Cessna 182H VP-YXZ on PRAW duties. It was on display at the May 1972 Centenary Air Show, with B.S.A.P. insignia on the vertical stabiliser. (Photo by Robin D. W. Norton)

Les Jellicoe, Harvey Middleton, Chips Owen, Bill Nightingale, Hennie Jooste, Ben Nieuwhoudt, Dougie Lyon and Gerry Cleveland. Members of the B.S.A.P. who flew with me as gunners were Inspectors Dave Young, Mike Tasker, Jan Weilopolski, Strydom, and Section Officer Chris Aitken.

After 73 hours, Hammy put his own aircraft into PRAW. Noel continued as my observer until he had completed 475 hours, after which he also flew as a PRAW pilot in his own right. I couldn't have wished for better observers and companions. Chips Owen then joined me, and we did many seven-day stints at the various FAFs.

In the early seventies, I had numerous interesting flights while flying Winston Hart of Special branch, to various places in Mozambique including several flights to Vuende, which was way north of the Zambezi River. Winston and I flew into several funny little strips along the Zambezi River. Sometimes the chef de post would be having his siesta so we would have to wait for him to wake up before Winston could interview him. Invariably they would serve us tasty snacks and Winston was able to enjoy a Manica beer or glass of wine.

One memorable training stint at Thornhill was climaxed by Noel and I being given a flight in a Vampire, as we had done quite well on the exercises we had flown. I think Colin Bickle and his observer were rewarded in the same manner. My pilot was Chris Dixon, of Green Leader fame. (Dixon led a raid on Zambia and became famous for his contact with Lusaka International tower and for controlling Zambian air space for the duration of the raid). Chris asked me what I would like to do and knowing that I would not have another opportunity to fly in a jet fighter I opted for some aerobatics. Unfortunately, the previous night was our last night at Thornhill so we had imbibed more than our normal amount of alcohol and just before landing, I was feeling distinctly queasy. The ground crews and the others were highly amused to see a somewhat white-faced individual climb out of the aircraft! Nevertheless, I was delighted at having had the chance to handle a jet.

In May 1974, Noel Waller and I were on a reconnaissance mission to the north of Chironga Mission. We spotted a terrorist camp situated on a kopje in a valley and decided to have a closer look so descended to about 800ft. Having confirmed our suspicions, we were climbing over some high ground when a sound like a swarm of bees started buzzing round us: this was followed by a stream of fuel pouring out of the port tank. Because of the thick timber, we were soon out of sight thus escaping from further small arms fire. I had made a habit of using one tank until it was dry and therefore knew how much flying time I had left in the remaining tank and had shortly before this switched on the port tank as the starboard tank was empty. As Todd`s law would have it the port tank was holed. Fortunately, being a high wing aircraft, by lifting the port wing sufficient fuel drained across to the starboard tank to get us back to the old airstrip at Mount Darwin. We had to get help to push XZ back to the threshold as the engine cut soon after landing.

Operation SPLITSHOT was the code name for a pamphlet dropping operation. The pamphlets contained information which was supposed to gain the "hearts and minds" of the Africans living in the TTLs (Tribal Trust Lands) thus gaining their support for the Government of the day and turning them against the terrorists. To get the pamphlets to land in the village we had to fly at about 400ft and at a slow speed, I didn't like this idea too much as there were bound to be terrs in some of the villages, and sure enough on one occasion we were met by a hail of small arms fire, fortunately only one bullet hit the aircraft.

Cessna 185 outside Aviation Services hangar, at the then Mount Hampden Airport, in January 1971. The only reference to VP-YRP in PRAW records was that it was listed on the BASP Nominal Roll of Aircraft dated 1 March 1974. In the background is Cessna 182 VP-YWI at one time owned by Chipinga Garages (Pvt) Ltd, which where it may have been used for PRAW flights. (Robin D. W. Norton)

Wally Barton recalls that "On 1 September 1978, CTs (Communist terrorists) attacked our house and hangar, which was about 50 metres from the house. They broke into the hangar, riddled VP-YXZ with bullets then set her alight. Only a part of the tailplane and the engine was left. This was a devastating blow to me as this was the only aeroplane I had ever owned. Fortunately, the police authorities were able to obtain another Cessna 182 for me, registration ZS-IUX that I received on 12 October". (Photo by Wally Barton)

Chinamora TTL Inspector Dave Young had been flying with me on the odd recce and to get some practice with the Browning. On 27 May 1978, a call sign, probably PATU, were in an O.P. in Chinamora TTL when they spotted seven CTs sitting outside a hut. Bindura Police called Dave and me in to react to the sighting. Bill Ludgater opted to go ahead of us. As soon as the terrs saw Bill`s aircraft they high-tailed it to the nearby bush, and we were unable to see them. Meanwhile, unbeknownst to us, PATU saw the terr`s run off and they set off in pursuit. We were orbiting the area and saw figures running through the bush. We were about to open fire, but in the nick of time spotted the dayglow on their hats, thus avoiding a nasty incident.

On our way back to Mt Darwin we were diverted to an ambush, which had taken place in Chessa purchase area East of Mt Darwin. On the way we came under fire, Dave returned fire, but by now it was too dark, so we returned to base. Noel, Les, and I had Wing Commander Peter Petter-Bowyer fly with us on two occasions to give us tips on recce work. Over the years we found many terrorist camps, several which could not be checked, in many cases due to the lack of troops to react. I was fascinated with aerial tracking and believe the hunting trips I went on were a help. We also found the camp run by PB at Rusape, where we were given instruction on recce: very helpful

Gerry Cleveland was flying with me as a gunner/observer while doing a week's stint at Buffalo Range on 21 August 1978, where we were liaising with an army unit. They tasked us to proceed to an area where the terrs had been active. We were able to find tracks of a group of about 14 in number. Tracking conditions were favourable, and we were able to follow the tracks for 30km. We realised the tracks were leading to a farm compound, so we stopped following and returned to base where we reported to the army unit. They carried out a follow-up exercise the next day, but unfortunately the terrs had not stopped at the first compound but had continued resulting in a failed exercise.

Twelve days later Chief Inspector Mike Tasker called me in for a briefing. Chris Aitken who had flown with me a few times to get some firing practice with the Browning, was to be my gunner. Mike had information to the effect that 30 terrs were having a meeting under a large tree at a specific grid reference. This was near the Musingwa river south of Kaitano. Mike instructed us to fly to the grid reference, to liaise with ground troops if any were available, if there were no troops, we were to attack the terrs with our single Browning. We found the large tree without any difficulty and as we approached the terrorists ran off, crossing an open patch of ground heading towards some dense riverine cover. Chris immediately opened fire, two of them went down. Having gained better cover the terrs returned fire in no uncertain manner, we continued orbiting and firing into the bush.

Mike Tasker, flown by Jim Barker, was also orbiting overhead looking for terrs. They soon spotted some crossing the river and Mike called us over. However, by this time we had sighted a group of about 12 running along a path heading south. Being the month of October there was not much leaf on the trees, so we had no difficulty following them. We started orbiting and Chris opened fire, one fell back, turned round, and started heading north. A second turned round and followed. We felt pretty sure they were wounded so we followed them. They went to ground under a large tree next to a dry stream, where Chris was able account for them. We then headed back to where Mike and Jim had seen another group of terrs crossing the river but had had to leave the scene. We then spotted a lone terr trying to conceal himself by standing next to a tree; I imagine he must have been wounded. As we were about to engage him, a call sign which had arrived on the scene a few minutes earlier requested us to clear some thick bush ahead of them. In retrospect we should have made them wait a few minutes. Anyway, we cleared the bush and then directed them to collect the two bodies. By now, we had run out of ammo. We decided to land at Kaitano, hoping that they might have some belts of ammo. While landing I discovered that only one brake was operating as the starboard brake had been damaged by gunfire. There was no ammo available, so we proceeded to Mukkers [Mukumbura] where we were resupplied with belts of ammo. We returned to the contact area but were unable to make any more sightings. The following day Jim Barker told me that he had recovered six bodies.

Harvey Middleton and I attended a four-day gunnery course at Katanga range, which was conducted by Bill Sykes. Three weeks later, on 22 November Hennie Jooste and I attended a second course and about this time, we were given twin Brownings.

Hennie Jooste and I were called out on the last day in January 1979, to assist Umvukwes PATU who were following up a bunch of terrs near Msonedi. Hammy Dax and another PRAW pilot were called on to orbit the area to try and spot in which direction the terrs would try to escape. Hennie and I located the PATU stick and then spotted two terrs about 500 metres ahead of the stick.

Alan Murry sold his Cessna Cardinal VP-WEEE and replaced it with a Cessna 210D VP-YOT, which was used by the SALOPS Flight and may have been armed. It is shown under cover in the Mashonaland Flying Club hangar in March 1972 (Robin D. W. Norton)

Wally (left) and Hennie Jooste (gunner, right) wearing flak jackets supplied by South Africa. The Cessna is armed with twin Brownings. (Photo by Wally Barton)

Hennie commenced firing and after several orbits the one terr was incapacitated and the second, who was wounded, hid in the bush. During one orbit we saw eight terrs standing under a tree at the base of the hill where PATU were waiting.

Unfortunately, we were unable to fire as PATU, although at a higher level, would have been directly in the line of fire. We had no option other than to withdraw and hope that PATU would be able to get a sighting. We took this opportunity to repair to Umvukwes to rearm. On our return to the area the terrs had vanished. PATU found the two injured terrs. I got a 'rocket' from Fire Force for not waiting for them, but by the time they arrived it was dark anyway.

On 12 February, Hammy Dax and I were tasked to search for occupied terrorist camps in the Kandeya TTL. We were given separate areas to recce and were to fly without our observers, which we had been doing for a while. Fire Force were on standby and were ready to react immediately. I reported finding a camp on a small kopje. An air force pilot checked the camp and decided it was unoccupied. About an hour later I found another camp where I saw movement. I called for the Fire Force who responded immediately, as the first chopper flew over, the terrs opened fire, sticks were dropped off and a contact ensued. By nightfall seven or eight terrs had been killed and the sticks took up ambush positions. During the night all sticks were withdrawn to enable them to be transferred to the Kariba area to conduct a follow-up after the shooting down of Air Rhodesia Viscount Flight 827, VP-YND Umniati.

Hennie Jooste and I had been on a follow-up in the Zambezi Valley to the north of Sipolilo and were returning to Mount Darwin on 20 March, when we received a call from B.S.A.P. Mount Darwin to the affect that Margaret Brooks had heard small arms fire coming from the tobacco lands near their farm boundary. She was worried about Len as he was believed to be in that area. We were asked to check the lands and soon found the vehicle and on closer inspection saw that Len was slumped over the steering wheel.

Having reported to Mount Darwin, we started searching for tracks which we found heading northeast towards the Ruia River. By this time, we had insufficient fuel left to go any further. We landed at FAF4 to refuel and debrief. We were tasked to continue tracking the next day. We picked up the tracks from the previous day and followed them to the Ruia River where we found a camp on the south bank of the river. We requested Fire Force to check for terrs. They came over and confirmed that it was a camp but the terrs had left. We then started a search to the north of the river, which put us in the Karuiana purchase area where after an extensive search, we picked up a strong track. I can`t remember how long this took, but all told we were airborne for 9 hours 15 minutes; we had refuelled at Mount Darwin.

Eventually the tracks bomb shelled which indicated that they were going to stop moving. Extending our orbits, we found a fairly well used camp just south of Tamandu farm in the Centenary area. We again requested Fire Force to check the camp as we were positive that the terrs had moved into the camp. They suggested that we use a motorcycle stick that was in the vicinity and were available in case of need. As soon as the motorcycle stick got close to the camp they were pinned down by withering fire from the terrorists. We contacted Fire Force and gave them the details of the contact, then flew over the camp to assist the unit on the ground. At this juncture the terrs left the camp and headed for a tributary of the Ruia. Hennie opened fire with the twin Brownings; I saw three of them go down and then get up again.

The remains of ZS-IUX with Derek Purnell (left) (VR Air force in charge of FAF Mt Darwin) and Ben Nieuwoudt (gunner). (Photo by Wally Barton)

Meanwhile we also came under fire with one round entering low down on the back of my seat and coming out near my right shoulder and exiting the cabin near the top air vent. We were searching for more targets in the riverine bush when Fire Force arrived and took over.

Gill Brown (Wally's daughter) stands next to Cessna 182P Skylane VP-WIV, which replaced ZS-IUX. (Photo by Wally Barton)

On this flight Ben Nieuwoudt (PATU stick leader) was my gunner as Hennie wasn't available. Ben often flew with me and was a crack shot with the Brownings, as was Hennie. Our brief on 28 September 1979, was to fly to an area south of Kaitano and search for a terr camp, which was said to be close to a village. Once we had located the camp Pookie Skeeles would come in with a Lynx and bomb the camp. We found the camp, which was situated in tall dense timber; as we orbited, the terrs came tearing out of the village heading for their camp where they had obviously left their weapons. They collected their weapons and 'bombshelled' out of the camp. Pookie was still a minute or two out, so we latched onto a single terr and Ben opened fire. I could see our tracer striking the ground right next to him. Without warning the engine died, not a cough or a splutter, nothing. We had descended to approximately 800ft, which was the height from which we normally fired.

A quick check of the instruments didn't indicate any problem. All I could do was turn away from the contact area, give Pookie a quick call to tell him that we were going down and then concentrate on landing into the trees more or less straight ahead which happened to be into wind. Shortly after hitting the trees a small clearing appeared; at this stage the nose wheel collapsed and for a moment I thought we wouldn't turn over as we were skidding along on the nose and slowing down rapidly, then the nose dug in, and we turned turtle. Neither of us was injured other than Ben having a small cut under one eye which he had stitched when we returned to Mt Darwin. After evacuating the inverted aircraft, we removed the Brownings and set them up next to an ant bear hole. I always carried an FN rifle and Ben had a 9mm pistol. My mouth was totally dry from the stress, so I risked a quick trip to the aircraft to collect water and sandwiches. Ben and I took up positions sitting back-to-back in the hole and prepared to wait for events to develop.

Meanwhile Pookie was chasing the gooks around and dropping his bombs, he was also able to get another aircraft to radio back to FAF4 to inform them of our predicament. Being lower than the escarpment he didn't have direct coms with base. Our police radio and the aircraft radio were both *US* so we were in the dark as to what was happening. After about an hour we heard two choppers approaching, I think they were flown by SAAF pilots. They dropped two sticks of Rhodesian Light Infantry (RLI) troopies who quickly deployed into the bush. While I was trying to recover the police radio, one chopper pilot uplifted Ben leaving me behind, however Ben soon got him to land again to pick me up. The sound of those choppers was most welcome. It was lucky for us that Fire Force had returned to Mt Darwin, after a prolonged absence.

Prior to the arrival of my next aircraft, VP-WIV, I flew as an observer for Bundu. One incident I remember well was our finding a camp in Karuyana Purchase area, which the B.S.A.P. decided to attack on 1 December. We were to control the troops, which consisted of a stick of territorials (I think) who were based at Swan base, which was a police outpost on Denis and Jackie Watsons farm in the Centenary East area. The other stick was made up of other personnel who were based at the camp.

The territorials approached the gook camp and found they had just left. We sighted the terrs from the air; they were heading north and were going to cross a road where the second stick was waiting. We tried to get them to cut off the terrorists, but they couldn't position themselves in time. The terrs realised they were being pursued so they bomb shelled and started running, heading for the Karuiana river and Kandeya TTL beyond. Cover being rather sparse the territorials could see them and opened fire from long range but without success. Bundu and I started following two of the terrs who were sticking together. After crossing the river, they headed north towards a school. They then passed a school they turned east and again crossed the river after which they turned southeast and started following the river line staying in the riverine timber. Bundu was passing this info to the pursuing army call sign, which set up a successful ambush.

Shortly after taking delivery of my new aircraft, VP-WIV, I was doing a solo recce below the escarpment in the Chiswiti area on 7 December, when I picked up tracks crossing a dry riverbed. On descending for a closer look, the terrs opened fire on me, but this time I had enough height to dive steeply and get out of range in a hurry. Not far off I found a camp, which I duly reported to B.S.A.P. Mt Darwin. I refrained from reporting a hole in one wing!

In tribute to my wife Erica, as a farmer's wife living at the 'sharp end', bordering on Kandeya Tribal Trust Land, in those troubled times: I can't say enough in praise of my dear wife, Erica, who had to help with the running of the farm during my frequent absences away on PRAW flying duties, often for a week at a time. She also had the risky job of going out at night with our manager, or cook, James, to place a few hurricane lamps or a vehicle with the lights on, to mark the runway for me whenever I flew in after dark. These were but two of the many things that were required of her and, finally, for staying married to me for almost 60 years!

Fire Force

Fire Force was the term used to describe a unique Rhodesian tactic to overwhelm the enemy through the rapid deployment of helicopter borne troops, paratroopers, and ground attack aircraft.

A Fire Force would be called in when contact was made with the enemy, through ambush, farm attacks, or when small four-man patrol units called for reinforcements.

The assault would be led by an Alouette III SA316B, K-car gunship, armed with a Matra MG 151 20mm cannon. The gunner would fire bursts of up to three rounds, of the 200 to 400 onboard. Each round was downrated to reduce the recoil for Alouette operations. A K-car was crewed by the pilot, the technician/

Elements of a Fire Force, a C-47 and three Aérospatiale *Alouette III helicopters on standby at a FAF5 Mtoko.* (Photo by John Frame)

A Fire Force ground attack Reims Cessna FTB 337G Lynx, armed with two Browning .303-inch machine guns in pods, mounted above the centre wing section and fitted with hard points for the delivery of FRANTAN, SNEB rockets or 'golf' bombs with the 3-metre probe to ensure they exploded above ground. (Photo by John Frame)

Rhodesian African Rifles (RAR) emplane for another Fire Force operation. The paratroopers of the RAR and RLI are known to have made up to four combat jumps in a day. (Photo by John Frame)

of 16 paratroopers would be dropped by a Douglas C-47 from 500 feet to clear the area.

The RLI and the RAR, both formidable bush-fighting regiments, along with national service units provided the ground forces. Heavily armed with at least one MAG per four-man stick, grenades and often 30lbs of ammunition, they fought in camouflage T-shirts and shorts, wearing trainers/running shoes, and carrying water, basic medical kits and minimal rations. Towards the end of the conflict, it was not unknown for the troops to make up to three combat jumps a day.

gunner, and positioned in the rear-facing front seat, the Fire Force Commander. In close formation would be three Alouette G-cars, with a crew of two and four fully equipped troops. To improve troop deployment the doors were removed, and the front seats set faced backwards. The technician/gunner would provide cover from the port rear door with an FN 7.62mm MAG machine gun using a Collimateur Lightweight Reflector Sight. The fitting was upgraded over time to include a spent cartridge holder, a padded chest plate and twin handgrips along with a Britiline fire limiter to prevent accidental damage to the airframe. Later the MAG was replaced by twin Browning Mk 2 .303-inch machine guns.

Initially the helicopters were supported by Percival Provost T52 trainers fitted with a pair of under-wing Browning .303-inch machine guns and on hard points 63mm SNEB rockets and FRANTANs, the locally made napalm bombs. From 1976 these were supplemented with the rather disappointing Aermacchi AL60-B2L Trojans. Both were replaced by 21 Reims Cessna FTB 337G Lynxes, twin-boom, push-pull piston-engines, light attack aircraft.

Once the troops were on the ground the helicopters would circle the action at 800 feet firing as directed and, supported by the ground attack unit, would attempt to close off escape routes. A sweep group

Pre-flight inspection on Cherokee 6 VP-WEL by Reserve Pilot Roy Anderson. The peak of Mt Darwin can be seen in the background. (Photo by Bill Linfield)

Gerry Cleveland: Copper 170[2]

I had just transferred from PATU to the PRAW and was required to team up with Roy Anderson who owned a Cherokee. He was to show me how PRAW operate out at a forward airfield. In this instance it was Fort Victoria. On this day we had to do a recce along the Lundi River, south of Buffalo Range, looking for human tracks in the riverbed. There was a police officer along with us because he knew the area.

We took off from Fort Victoria and reached the Lundi about 30 minutes later and started our circular sweep gradually working downstream in an easterly direction. The weather was fine, and the sun angle was just right so any tracks would have immediately stood out. We were operating at about 1,000 feet. We droned round and round and round not saying very much as the various farmsteads, with their identifications painted on their roofs, came into and out of our field of view. So far, we had not seen any tracks and the conversation dwindled.

Roy decided that we might see more of we did this recce low level. So down we went to about 200 feet. We certainly saw much more but the distraction of the riverbank with its trees and the possibility of gooks waiting until we got into the perfect shot position was foremost on my mind.

So, we droned on for another few minutes before it happened. There was a hell of a bang, which woke us all up uttering all sorts of expletives. Yes, those Post Office guys, and their damn pieces of wire hung across the river got us right on the propeller spinner. The plane yawed violently to the right as the wire dragged along the right wing then ripped into the wing tip tank. Plane still flew okay, and Roy elected to divert to Buffalo Range airport to assess the damage. On landing we found that the spinner was torn, and the leading edge of the starboard wing had deep scoring. The wing tip tank was leaking and needed some extensive repair work.

Type Conversion Cessna 210

As part of my usefulness in PRAW, I was trained to fly the Cessna 210. When my instructor considered that I was safe enough to take the test, Tony Weeks, an Air Rhodesia instructor arrived at Charles Prince for the test.

Graham Keith's C210 had been pre-flighted by me, with Tony asking all sorts of questions about the aircraft during the pre-flight inspection. With the fuel on board, we needed an extra passenger to bring the weight up to max so one of the staff of Skyline Charters volunteered.

Tony wanted me to demonstrate a short field take off. I set the flaps to 15, brakes on, applied full power. Brakes off and kept the plane pointing down 06 runway. Rudder applied enough to keep straight. On reaching IAS 60 knots, I pulled back and we lifted off and accelerated straight ahead with gear away once past any usable runway then eased off the flap while still climbing to 6,500 feet. We were cleared to SD4 training area, to do all the manoeuvres, stalls, steep turns, incipient spin, setting up the plane for max range cruise and other fuel saving settings.

The next stage was to demonstrate how to lower the undercarriage with a simulated failure of the hydraulic pump. Having selected gear down, I pumped the emergency pump and heard the nose wheel unlock. Then the main gear started to come down. Then everything stopped coming down. Tony took over the pumping while we tried to recycle the procedure. The main wheels were still dragging along behind, and we realised that the next landing was going to be a wheels-up arrival.

I called the tower to advise them of our predicament and I elected to land on the grass alongside RWY06. Meanwhile Alan Kearns who was airborne doing training volunteered to come over and have a look. He said that there was red hydraulic oil coming from the left-side wheel area and streaking down the fuselage. By now, we were talking through the forced landing procedure.

Unlock the doors and brief everyone that once the plane stops to open the doors and step away from the plane. Rig plane for landing and chose the area of grass on the left side of the runway. Final approach with 30 degrees flap, mixture rich, prop fine. Round out with zero power and mags off with prop stopped. Tried to crank prop so no blade would strike ground. We skidded about 50 yards with wings level. Turned off all electric power and abandoned ship to safe distance on either side.

When the aircraft was recovered to Skyline's hangar and up on jacks, DCA engineers inspected the undercarriage to find that a circlip on the left main door had popped, allowing the end to come out with subsequent loss of all fluid.

No Lights at Nyamapanda Police Post

It was Saturday afternoon, 18 December 1979; I was still in PATU but had been accepted as a PRAW pilot. Sue and I were excited to be going to the B.S.A.P. Christmas Ball that evening. We had decided to team up with our PATU and Air Wing friends. Tony Eldridge had reserved a table and we were to meet at 7:30 pm for a few drinks in the *Copper Pot* (the Police Pub) before dinner. The Police Prison band had been booked with their lively group of fantastic instrumentalists.

I was in my workshop getting something fixed for our caravan that we were taking to Jacana Yacht club for a few days with the kids and some relaxing sailing. Sue called me around 3 p.m. to say that Chief Inspector Fred Pringle from PGHQ was on the phone.

Fred had an urgent request from the Nyamapanda Police post asking for two Police Pioneer maintenance electricians to be flown out urgently. Early the previous morning, the police post had been attacked with RPG's, which disabled the lights, and the diesel generator had shut down. The generator refused to start again. The police on site could not find the problem and had asked for urgent assistance.

The request was to fly the maintenance team to Kotwa airfield where we would be met and taken on by road to Nyamapanda, which was the border post with Mozambique on the road to Tete and Malawi. RUAC had their Cessna 210 Centurion ZS-EWD fuelled up ready to go from their hangar at Salisbury Airport. Fred said it was probably a broken wire or something simple and that we would be home in a couple of hours! Yeah! Yeah! Fred had arranged for the Pioneer team to be at the plane and had alerted Flight Information Centre of the call out.

I got that second-hand look (again) from Sue. She knew that I could not get there have the problem fixed and be back for the party she had so looked forward to. She had made a new dress for the occasion.

A police B-car picked me up from the house and rush me out to Salisbury Airport. What an exciting trip that was – haring through Salisbury with sirens going and lights flashing! Barging through traffic lights and arriving at RUAC on an adrenalin high with a pulse rate to match.

I had phoned my flight plan through and spoken to Met Office for an *en-route* forecast – nothing serious but scattered thunderstorms to the North of Mazoe, Concession and Bindura and in the Shamva area. I planned to go out VFR low level on a direct route via Mtoko.

After I had completed the pre-flight inspection, we loaded a large toolbox and got the experts comfortably seated: we started up and taxied out to runway 06 holding point. The ADF-needle indicated active thunderstorms ahead. After takeoff, I could see that there was a significant build up to the north, but along my track, it was easy going. If we could get the job done in an hour, we could have an easy flight back and be in time for the party.

There were no nav-aids on route, so I had the VOR and ADF set to the Salisbury nav-aids. We flew out low level to Kotwa airfield and had a smooth ride. Overhead Kotwa we made comms with the police detail who was to drive us to Nyamapanda Police outpost. The Patrol Officer had posted a constable with his trusty FN as guard for RUAC's expensive Cessna 210 while he drove us to Nyamapanda.

My job as the PRAW pilot was half done and I thought I would be standing around for a few minutes while the electricians spotted and fixed the defect and got power restored. After about an hour and still no signs that the problem had been found, I began to be concerned about the constable guarding the plane in the approaching dusk, a night takeoff from an unlit runway, and the feeling that I might not get back to the party after all.

I watched the electricians start the diesel generator and watched it come up to speed only to see it shut down again because of an excessive load. By now, it was getting dark and wondered if I should head back to the plane and fly to Mtoko for the night. As I pondered the dilemma, I wandered outside while the electricians restarted the engine – again. As it got up to speed, I saw a big flash high up on the security fence. The generator output was being shorted where the power lines crossed the fence. An insulator on the power lines had been hit by an ASK round or RPG and the lines had sagged down onto the chain link fence and tripped the system. The electricians replaced the insulator, and they started the generator. By now, it was dark and I wondered how I would get out of Kotwa airfield.

We got back to the airfield at Kotwa around 6pm. There were no available lights for a flare path, and we were not happy about spending a night at Kotwa with the plane at the airfield. So, in true Rhodesian 'let's make a plan' style, we all climbed aboard the police Land Rover and drove down the runway looking for anything that might be a problem. All seemed okay so I instructed the constable to drive to the far end of the runway and face us as with his side lights on as we rolled down on our take off run. With the plane's landing lights, we could make out the edges of the runway and we were soon up and heading back to Salisbury. I contacted Salisbury Information and asked for Special VFR clearance, which was stretching it a bit because we could not see the ground. They gave us the clearance and we climbed to 7,500 feet.

I had a commercial pilot licence without an instrument rating, but had many hours training with Peter Wilson, a DCA instructor and PRAW pilot. As we approached Mrewa, I could see that the thunderstorms had moved southwards, down towards the city and it was raining hard with very spectacular lightning. I knew I could not get back to the airport on a direct track. Instead, I used the Mazoe Non-Directional Beacon (NDB) [ADF beacon] to route around and behind the storm.

After a bumpy ride with lots of lightning, we eventually made it behind the weather and safely made it back to the airport. Sue and I arrived at the Police Ball about an hour late and found that our party had been briefed by Fred Pringle. The drinks were ready, and the music was great.

A Note About Night Flying

When you have 1,000 foot clearance, at least three miles horizontal visibility and can keep clear of cloud during a night flight, you can ask for Special Visual Flight clearance. However, this is not normally granted when the weather is bad. We complied with these requirements as we left Kotwa but not as we approached Salisbury Airport. Chuck Drake was the Radar Controller on duty that night and he had been briefed that a PRAW flight might be returning from the east. Chuck steered me around the worst parts of the weather and helped me to final approach for runway 06. I think he really reduced my heart rate with his assuring assistance.

A Very Successful Mission

We used to be called out by SALOPS Ops Centre from our places of work for air support duties and this meant that we had to be able to drop what we were doing and head out to the airfield where our Cessna 206 was parked. From the time we were called to the time we got airborne, perhaps 45 minutes had passed. Often by then the whole scene had changed and our efforts would be quite useless.

Chief Inspector Fred Pringle provided a wooden shed for us alongside the main hangar at Charles Prince Airport. He also had a scramble phone installed. In this shed, we had a table and a few magazines where we could sit and wait to be called. The plane would be parked outside fuelled, pre-flighted and ready to go at a moment's notice. Reaction time was reduced to minutes, which meant we could be overhead an incident within about 20 minutes of a call out.

On this one occasion my observer, Paul Chappe and I had been sitting kicking our heels, updating our maps when the phone rang. Got airborne for provided map reference where there was a contact in progress. The call sign on the ground was Mantle 40.

We had an arrangement with Des Anderson and the other ATC controllers for priority clearance when we were scrambled, which worked quite well when the traffic was light. We taxied down to the holding point for runway 06 and while I did my pre-take off checks and once airborne and clear of the circuit we contacted Salisbury Radar on 119.1 and gave the rough area we would be working in and the height then over to SALOPS on 122.3 for an up-to-date briefing. The radio relay Lima Alpha in the Dombashawa area was already in contact with Mantle 40 and told us that the contact was about 15 minutes previous and that they were following tracks up a hill feature towards higher ground.

Some minutes later, we were overhead and in contact with the call sign who said that they were on a routine patrol through the kraal line when they were suddenly fired on by about five insurgents who had been feeding in the kraal. Fire was returned and the shooting stopped.

We went into our elliptical right-hand orbit with me now sitting in the right-hand seat and Paul looking over the MAG out of the cargo door on the right side. It wasn't long before we picked up a well-worn path that headed northwards along a valley and stream that disappeared into a tree line. The Mantle call sign followed the general line of the path in the direction we indicated, we searched ahead for physical signs of the enemy. We were quite sure that they were hotfooting it away from the contact area under the cover of the trees. I asked Paul to do a probe with fire into the tree line and sure enough after a few minutes we hear that familiar sound like hail hitting the windscreen in a bad thunderstorm. Fire was being returned from the trees.

The Mantle call sign was close behind and when they heard the shooting from the tree line, they were not too keen to continue because of the danger of an ambush. We agreed a plan where they would take up a defensive position and watch the path into the trees and we would try to flush out the opposition towards them.

We probed the trees again with gunfire, and this time there was heavy fire returned and we could see smoke in the trees and guessed that this was the gooks location. The gunner poured some accurate fire into the smoke and we were surprised to see a number of fairly large explosions. The

Paul Chappe and Gerry Cleveland with the trophy they won at the last fly-in sponsored by the Air Force at Thornhill. This was a two-day event where RhAF judged us on all aspects of our abilities. (Photo by Gerry Cleveland)

firing stopped while we continued to orbit the site. We asked the Mantle call sign to resume follow-up while we continued along the direction of flight. The tree line started to break up along what was a strong stream and from the bush we could see two gooks in camouflage running hard between clumps of trees heading along the side of the stream. We called for a stop line to be put in across the line of flight and asked the Mantle to get into the tree line to follow-up. This they reluctantly did. While coordinating the placement of the stop line we lost sight of the fleeing gooks. There was no cover away from the streamline so they could not have gone far.

Eventually the follow-up call sign came to the site of the explosions and described the scene as body pieces, camo uniforms, AKs and grenades. They estimated that here were three deceased CTs. We urged the call sign to speed up their follow-up as we were down to an hour's fuel remaining. The stop line was in position when the Mantle stick came to the clearing where we lost the two gooks. Mantle 04 could not see tracks where we indicated.

We orbited while wondering just where they had gone. We pointed out a couple of pools in the stream and suggested that Mantle 04 fire a few rounds into the water. Up the two gooks came. They had crawled into the reeds in the deep end of the pool.

Duped by Radio Call

Lima Alpha called us while we were on recce looking for gook tracks in the Chinamora TTL. The report was that there was a Mantle call sign calling but they could hardly make out what they were saying.

We flew across to the area indicated by LA [Lima Alpha] and spoke with the Mantle stick who said their radio battery was failing and could we drop another to them. We did not carry spare batteries for the A30 radio but asked them to talk us overhead. Their signal was poor and fading, almost as though we were a long way from them.

With the Becker homer in the aircraft, we got a position line towards them then the signal faded out altogether. A couple of days later Lima Alpha said that the unknown Mantle stick was again trying to make contact. We managed to raise them and with the Becker, homing device got another position line on them. So, we flew at right angles to this position line and asked them to transmit again. We got another position line and it seemed as though they seemed to be transmitting from Zambia somewhere. Paul had drawn these lines on our map. Now we understood why the signal was so poor. Was this a bogus call from someone claiming to be a friendly in the hopes that we might be suckered?

We received no feedback to our sitrep.

Buffalo Range

At the time of this incident, I was one of four Assistant Chief Telecommunications Technicians, and my immediate boss was Jonah Jones, the Chief Telecomms Tech and we worked out of the DCA offices on the 11th floor of the Earl Gray building in Salisbury. On one of my visits to Buffalo Range airport with some electronics technicians from Salisbury Airport, we had to repair the VHF comms system (again).

We had flown down in the DCA's Cessna 206, VP-YAA, loaded with test equipment and spares and were going to be on site a couple of days as we soon found out with the problems we found.

At around 1300, I was contacted by the local FAF and asked if I would come over for a chat. There, in the bush camp just off the runway, I was introduced to the local SB inspector. He said he had been on to Chief Inspector Fred Pringle who was I/C PRAW at PGHQ looking for an aircraft fitted with a homing device.

Fred found out that I was down at FRBR and that the aircraft that we were using may be fitted with such a device, which it was. This was an indicator using a vertical pointer that gave a steering indication left or right of the aircraft's heading to steer towards a VHF transmission. We used this to find our troops on the ground if they pressed the transmitter key on their VHF radio set. Or, as it turned out in this case, a clandestine source of VHF signal. The homing device was a local crib of the Becker Homer and was made by Howard Benjamin at his Avionics shop at Charles Prince Airport just outside Salisbury.

The SB detail then asked if I was prepared to go on a gook hunt and briefed me on the task. About 60 miles south of the airport, some gooks had broken into a local store and stolen food and a radio. This they often did because our news broadcasts on FM used to include up-to-date reporting on terrorist activity in various areas in the country. Unbeknown to the gooks, some of the radios on sale in the rural stores had been doctored by the police radio unit where Chief Inspector Dave Todden was in charge. These experts had fitted miniature VHF transmitters to some radio sets and used the carting handle as the antenna. When the radio was turned off, the transmitter would turn on and radiate a tone-coded signal. Fortunately, the radio stolen was one of these.

I left the team on the job on the excuse that I had to go down to fetch someone from a bush airfield and would not be back until that evening. We took off and climbed out to the south towards the last known position of the gooks as reported by the trackers who, on the ground were following their spoor.

About 40 minutes into the flight, we heard the very faint beeping of the radio signal coming from the radio. Not enough to give an indication yet but certainly enough for us to determine that the signal was getting stronger. We climbed higher. As a result, the homer started showing signs of interest. I changed heading until the homer showed that the aircraft was pointing towards the source. From the ground, a casual observer would see a light aircraft flying in a straight line and would think that this was just another farmer going somewhere.

Meanwhile in the aircraft we had our 1:250 map out and were drawing a track line from visual references on the ground. As soon as we had flown overhead the source, the homer indicated a needle reversal, and we marked the position and flew on for another 10 minutes. While we were doing this, we contacted Rutenga FAF and briefed them on our progress and that we would land there later with our results.

We gradually circled around until we were heading back to the source but this time at right angles to our original track all the while hoping that the signal would keep coming. As we flew back towards the source of the radio transmission, the homer eventually indicated that we were overhead. We marked our map and noted that the signal was coming from a river line that was clearly visible. Once again, we continued for 10 minutes, which, at our speed, was about 30 miles, while we contacted FAF Rutenga again, telling them we had information and would proceed to their location.

Group Captain Robbie Gaunt was the FAF commander and he had been doing some pre-planning for the cause. He had several choppers with Fire Force and a DC3 with RLI parachute troops on board all about to depart to Fort Vic FAF. Robbie decided to delay their departure for a couple of hours and had briefed them on what we had been up to.

We landed and all we really had to do was to show them where we had found the gooks. I was asked to fly low-level tracking ahead of the Fire Force who were following along behind in the choppers and the parabats above at 2,000 feet in the DC3. When we arrived over the site, the signal was still strong, so we knew that at least the radio was there. Fire Force then took charge while we got out of the way.

Fire Force flew up the river line over the site but still could not see anyone in the bush. I was called back in to fly across the site and indicate when we were directly overhead. Down to 50 feet now and weaving along the trees towards the signal. We called out "overhead" as we flew out of the fire zone.

Some of the choppers landed and the Fire Force deployed to sweep through the area. Soon we heard what we had hoped to hear, "Contact, Contact, Contact." I then flew back to Rutenga to refuel and wait for the heroes to return for the debriefing.

The SB detail was anxious to recover the radio that the gooks had stolen from the store. One of the RAR Fire Force team had picked it up and had claimed it as a wartime trophy. He was not about to let it out of his sight without some serious bargaining. He wanted to know why he should give it up but of course, he couldn't be told. So a deal was made. He was promised a brand-new radio with all sorts of features and costing many times the value of the radio SB wanted.

Instrument Rating Test

By now my IF training with Peter Wilson was progressing well and he considered that I was ready for my IF test. My confidence was improving with each training session and now I was ready for the dreaded flight test.

Somehow, I pulled the short straw and my DCA examiner turned out to be Tony Birch who was a nice person but was known to be very strict. Since I also worked for the DCA, I guess they wanted to be sure I was not going to break their Cessna 206, VP-YYA. They must have decided to send Tony out to make sure.

At RUAC's hangar at Salisbury Airport, the pre-flight seemed to take hours and I had the instrument approach charts for Salisbury readily available. Tony's briefing was very clear. "Please relax and pretend that you are taking your grandmother for a ride. There will be nothing out of the ordinary on this short test." This reminded me of my cross-country exam for my commercial licence. Tony was the examiner, and he used the same sentence.

So, I put up the screens across the left side of the windscreen and left window so that with the hood I was to wear, I couldn't see out.

We taxied out under Tony's guidance, left a bit, right a bit, straight, all the way down to the run-up area for Rwy 06. Did the run-up checks and lined up on the runway. I aligned the DI to the magnetic compass. Called Tower (118.1) for TO clearance and applied power. Corrected swing with rudder all the while keeping the DI on the runway heading. After lift-off, retracted flaps and set power for climb speed while maintaining runway heading.

Called Radar (119.1) for clearance towards Bromley (BZ on ADF).

Part of the test was called limited instrument flying. Certain of the flight instruments were blanked out with cardboard, I was left with airspeed, altimeter, turn and bank, and the magnetic compass was very different to what I had done in my training. I had to cage the gyro-operated direction indicator then Tony took control. It felt like he threw the plane into all sorts of attitudes and airspeeds. Then asked me to recover using what instruments were available to me. This went on and on and on until I was beginning to get quite nauseous.

During some of these manoeuvres Tony would create some distraction as an extra problem for me to handle. On one occasion as the aircraft was on the point of stall, he applied a boot full of rudder and away we went into a spin. Incipient spins were also on his list.

Eventually when he had run out of ideas, he told me to enter the letdown procedure for an ILS approach from BZ. I remember asking Tony if he would take control while I recovered my approach plate from the floor. "No way," he said, "I am your grandmother who doesn't know how to fly a plane."

By now, I was getting thoroughly irritated with the whole carry-on. Somehow, I did manage the approach and landing. We taxied back to RUAC's hangar and shut down. I angrily took down the screens, opened to door and was about to climb out. As I was about to climb out, Tony said, "Wait a minute, we need to debrief." I can't remember much about the debrief, except that he was quite happy with the test and that I had passed.

Later during my flying-career, I realised that Tony was pushing my envelope and that this would benefit me on a night flight back from Bulawayo to Charles Prince. As I turned finals for runway 14 and switched on the landing lights, there was a total electrical failure. No lights, no radio, no instrument lights, no flaps. There was an aircraft waiting to enter Rwy 14 and I could see his lights. This helped me determine where the runway threshold was. I parked the plane and went up to the tower to find Des Anderson on duty.

Lost at Night

During one of my 2-week stint at Rutenga military base using a Cessna 182 belonging to the Mashonaland Flying Club, I was tasked with a simple flight, taking a VIP to Fort Victoria military base located on the east side of runway 35 threshold, then return in time to enjoy the camp movie.

We departed at around 18:00 and headed 355 magnetic in overcast weather to Fort Vic. No problem, because the ADF gave me a good bearing on FRFV NDB. Smooth flight landed and dropped off my passenger at the Military Camp on the airfield at dusk.

Taxied out for takeoff around 19:00 and by now it was getting dark. I had an instrument rating so did not anticipate a problem getting back to Rutenga. The Rutenga railway marshalling yard was equipped with very bright lights, which were not on, but it wasn't a problem because the ADF gave me good bearing lines on FV and Messina. The only other NDB was CZ at Chiredzi, which I was not using. There had been talk of a transmitter operating from Mozambique on the same frequency as Chiredzi's NDB with the intention of drawing traffic and attempt to shoot them down.

The flight time from FRFV to Rutenga was about 40 minutes and I should have been able to see the base camp lights when about 10 minutes out. After 40 minutes, there were no sign of Rutenga. I called then and asked for the rail yard light to be switched on. They said the lights were already on. I realised that I was not sure of my position but had fuel to get back to Fort Vic if I didn't sort myself within the next 15 minutes. An army call sign came up on the radio and said that he had heard an aircraft fly nearby about 5 minutes ago. He identified their position way to the east of my intended track. Now I really started to feel lonely. I did not relish the idea of landing on a road or even in the trees at night.

The guys at Rutenga were having a movie outdoors on the big screen they had set up in the trees. The 'voice' at the Rutenga radio changed to one of the air force pilots who asked me about my in-flight conditions. I was VFR below cloud. He said they would fire off a parachute flare, which gives an intense white light. I saw the flare burning way off to the east of my position. After I landed, I was greeted by the camp commander and after a debriefing, he then recommended that I buy the folks a round from the pub.

Next morning several 'experts' including myself gathered around the plane and threw ideas at each other. Then one of the air force technicians leant into the plane and turned on the instrument lights. Only when he added the compass light did the compass bearing change greatly. That morning we all learnt something that was so simple and should be part of our pre-flight inspection especially if there is night flying involved. The wiring to the magnetic compass was creating a magnetic field around the compass that affected the reading by about 20 degrees. The wires to the compass light should be tightly twisted all the way to the compass. The current through the twisted pair of wires tends to cancel the magnetic field and so not affect the compass bearing. The compass light wiring was not twisted but just ran up alongside the vertical metal windscreen divider to the compass

Marymount Mission

I was doing a stint at I think FAF Mtoko, when I was requested to remove all the seats from the C206 ZS-IYN that I was using, collect some blankets, and head for Marymount Mission at the request of the SB. I thought I was going to collect some bodies.

The short airstrip at this location runs east to west and the prevailing wind is generally from the east. However, this strip runs steeply downhill to the east ending up in a river valley followed by steep rising ground. So, the rule for was to land west and take off east, irrespective of wind direction. Landing up-hill for the newcomer is quite an experience. Instead of a powered descent as in a normal approach, one reduces speed in level flight while extending flaps. Maintain this attitude while approaching the end of the rising runway then start climbing to match the gradient and reduce the speed further. You should end up on the runway – if you got the plan right. Then back off the power enough to keep taxiing up the gradient.

After taxiing off the strip towards the swimming bath, I met the SB detail who took me to their HQ in the swimming bath changing room and showed me a huge pile of captured AK and SK weapons that he needed taken to their office at Mtoko by air. The situation at Marymount Mission was tense and there were still armed terrs in the area so SB could not go by road.

Many willing hands helped load the aircraft but with the need for speed, the rifles were just piled up into the aircraft somewhere around the c of g. The pile reached up above the windows. There was no tie down netting available. The cargo door was closed and the SB guy wished me luck. (Little did he know how I would need it).

Takeoff run downhill was okay with the aircraft accelerating well, but as I rotated the pile of weapons slid backwards on the floor. So did the C of G. I was now in a situation where I was climbing out of the river line with full power and full forward trim and I had to push hard on the control column to keep the aircraft from stalling.

There was no way I could drag any of the cargo forward with the plane in a climbing attitude while working my way up to a safe height. I was in that state of calm anxiety and running on full adrenalin, knowing that if the engine quit, then I and the plane would end up as a smudge in a remote TTL far from help.

Eventually I reached about 1,000 feet and tried to level off and get the speed up. The airspeed rose from the climb speed of 95kts to about 110kts and some of the load came off the control column, but I still had full nose down trim and full power. Any reduction in power just caused the situation to worsen.

Eventually I arrived at Mtoko some 20 minutes later and now had the interesting job of getting down in one lump. I warned FAF that I had a C of G shift and was manoeuvring with difficulty. Fortunately, Mtoko airstrip is another one of those sloping fields. I touched down going up-hill / down-wind with full power on and just a trickle of flap. Once on the ground I kept the power on and applied brakes just to keep the plane from sitting on its tail.

SB must have got on the horn during my flight because there was a guy waiting for me with a cargo net for my next trip.

PATU Support in Training Exercise

We were operating with five PATU sticks that were on a training exercise just north of Christon Bank, which is in the hilly ground south of Mazoe dam. It was a hot afternoon and we all wanted was to get to the Police pub, *The Copper Pot*. The PATU sticks were on open order in the low ground and moving south.

As we were droning around overhead, Paul, my observer saw what looked like someone on the high ground to the west in a cammo uniform squatting down. As we circled around the squatting figure looked like a gook having a crap. His AK rifle was on the ground next to him.

We immediately called the PATU lead section and told them what we saw. The response was that we were kidding. We assured them that this was a genuine call and further we had seen more gooks

A PATU briefing, from left to right: SO G. Westland, obscured unknown, PO R. J. Page, Inspector G. C. Campbell, Constable L. M. Tsveture, obscured unknown, PO C. W. Johnstone, Inspector G. A. Miller, Constable S. Mharadzi, PO C. J. Birtle, R/PO L. B. Tierney, PO W. L. B. (Billy) Egleton, unknown, Pilot unknown, obscured unknown. (B.S.A.P. Regimental Association)

hiding from our plane. It looked as if they were going to ambush the PATU sticks near a road just south of their current position.

Much disbelief from the sticks. Eventually SALOPS came up and instructed the PATU call signs to consider this a real call and to load up and investigate.

We had a call from a local Police Reserve stick that were very close to our 'contact area' so we asked them to form a stop line overlooking the road. When the PATU sticks were loaded up with live ammo, they changed direction and climbed into the high ground and proceeded south with extended flanks.

It wasn't long before we heard those magic words, 'Contact, Contact, Contact'. We never knew the result as the PATU sticks made comms with the Police Reserve stick and had a team debrief. Meanwhile we departed the scene and met up with everyone at the Copper Pot.

Troops from Kanyemba

I was doing my PRAW duty at Mt Darwin FAF using a Cessna 206 aircraft ZS-IYN belonging to Skyline Charters, when I was called by the ops section. I was asked to collect five soldiers from Kanyemba airfield and take them to Charles Prince Airport. The reported weather at the Kanyemba airfield was clear after some rain. Weather at Mount. Darwin was clear.

I decided my route would follow the road north then down the Alpha Trail down the Mavuradonha escarpment following the river to the Angwa River then follow that to Kanyemba airstrip. As soon as I got to the escarpment, I saw that Zambezi Valley was covered in low cloud. I could see the ground occasionally so decided to head for Mashumbi Pools, which I could find by following the Hunyani River northwards.

I found a place where I could descend below the cloud, which turned out to be 50 to 100 feet agl [above ground level], and followed the many tributaries down to where they joined the Hunyani. I soon saw the police camp at the Mashumbi Pools airstrip, but what surprised me was the number of other aircraft waiting there. I landed to find out that the planes were grounded due to fog. I remarked that the troopies at Kanyemba reported clear sky after some rain. Big smiles all round. The Mashumbi Pools Police said that the place was fogbound for days.

Around midday, the cloud base seemed to have lifted a little and I decided to head north along the Angwa River. After takeoff, I headed west low level and soon found the Angwa. I then followed the river north still low level (50 feet or so). Hopped over the bridge while looking out left for Kanyemba airstrip.

There was no clear sky, which annoyed me somewhat, and I resolved to tell my passengers that they had put my safety and the plane on the line by their lies. I found the field in the mist and landed. The troops were off on R & R and had I known about the fog, I wouldn't have made the trip. On the way south I climbed on instruments to around 7,000 feet to clear the escarpment. Everything was still in cloud.

I got my own back by simulating turbulent weather and bouncing the plane around considerably. Some of the troopies ended up by puking in their hats.

Mtoko

Once again Paul Chappe and I took off from FAF Mtoko with my favourite aircraft, C206 ZS-IYN of Skyline Charters, on a recce up over the top end of the Mazoe River where there had been reports of gook infiltration. Our job was to look for spoor.

What we did find was a very well developed local farming community of which our briefing officer was unaware. We marked it up on our 1:50 map. Could find nothing that looked like gook tracks because cattle and people had walked everywhere.

On our way back to Mtoko we got the message to divert to Nyakasoro airstrip where we had to casevac two wounded soldiers from the RAR (Rhodesian African Rifles) who had been in a firefight with some terrorists and bring them back to Mtoko for medical treatment.

We landed to find the whole company waiting for us. Paul and I removed the middle and rear seats and laid down a couple of mattresses that the troops had brought along from their base camp. The wounded soldiers were transferred from stretchers to the mattress somehow and we were all set to depart when the Sergeant-Major said they would like to sing the RAR song – Sweet Banana – in appreciation for our effort. They sang beautifully and with much feeling.

Cessna U.206F ZS-IYN, after restoration to a civilian finish, was parked at Frascati forward airfield on the runway, which was nothing more than a narrow path cleared in a reasonably straight line through the farmland. At times, a grenade launching device would be installed in the cargo pod fitted below the aircraft. The RhAF developed a grenade launcher for their Percival Provost aircraft, designed to deliver white phosphorous grenades when the aircraft undertook ground attacks. It was made of four separate banks into which the grenades were inserted, following removal of their safety pins, and then retained by a spring-loaded door for each bank. The opening of the doors and release of the grenades was managed via a switch box in the crew cabin. Loading and unloading of the pod was a very time-consuming and precarious procedure requiring somebody to lie underneath the aircraft and carefully insert or remove 40 grenades. It was only used on a few occasions and abandoned when a teargas grenade was dropped while unloading, causing havoc at Charles Prince Airport. (Photo by Tony Mann)

Clandestine Leaflet Drop at Night

During the ceasefire period prior to the 1980 elections for a new Government, in which Mugabe and Nkomo were candidates as per the Lancaster House Agreement.

The distribution of political party literature by the security forces to the indigenous people was prohibited by the elections committee, who were overseeing the electioneering process. The general feeling among the RSF was that the elections committee was skewed in favour of Mugabe and his ZANU PF party and were turning a blind eye to the rife intimidation that was taking place in the TTLs all over the country by gooks that were not in their special 'no go' camps.

The Rev. Abel Muzorewa, a known supporter of democracy, had negotiated with the Government for parallel ministerial seats in the legislature to introduce the majority to the envisioned democratic future. All this hard work was not about to be for naught.

I assumed that somehow or other there were people in high places that were not prepared to stand by while this rife intimidation was allowed to take place right under their noses and were hatching plans to level the playing fields.

Paul and I were called in to Chief Inspector Fred Pringle's office at PGHQ for a briefing. Fred knew that I had an instrument rating and had decided that because of Paul's and my PATU experience, we were the ones to do the job.

The task was clandestine in as much as we had to fly at night without exterior lights over the TTL North of Salisbury to drop leaflets and posters in support of the Reverend Abel Muzorewa and his democratic UANC party.

These leaflets would be brought out to our aircraft at Charles Prince Airport by an unmarked vehicle and the occupants would help us load the plane at the end of runway 06 after sunset. The aircraft VP-YYA, a Cessna 206, was owned by the Government and operated by the Department of Civil Aviation. I was a Senior Engineering Officer in the Department's radio branch and had clearance to fly this aircraft with my commercial licence and instrument rating.

The area that we were to operate in was part of the SALOPS zone. Our call sign as members of the SALOPS flight was Copper 281 and we were familiar with this area but our knowledge of the ground and its features would be of little help because the drop was planned for a moonless night. The exercise had to be done using what few radio aids were available, (VOR radio navigation aid (VSB) at Salisbury Airport, the low powered NDB at Mazoe (MZ) and another NDB (BZ) at a place called Bromley).

We worked out a series of points where position lines measured from the radio aids crossed at angles greater than 60 degrees. This would give us best accuracy over the TTL taking in to account the quadrennial errors of the ADF system and the VOR errors. We planned to use the Mazoe NDB MO on 363 KHz, Bromley NDB BZ on 284 KHz, Salisbury VOR on 113.1 MHz. As far as the Air Traffic Controllers were concerned, the flight was to be a cross-country

Ahead of the ceasefire, settlement and run-up to the general elections in 1980 all parties attempted to influence the electorate. The Rhodesian Government produced a series of posters. This is an example of the posters dropped by PRAW over towns and rural areas. (Photo by Alan Murray)

Another example of a pre-election poster warning that 'if you try to stop the people from voting, you will be going against the will of the people, and the Zimbabwe People's Army WILL kill you'. (Photo by Alan Murray)

PRAW navigational exercise at 7,000 feet followed by a diversionary night landing before heading back to Charles Prince Airport.

At sundown, we loaded the 206 with leaflets and posters. To accommodate the load, we had to remove all seats except the driver's seat and centre right seat where Paul would sit. Dispersal was to be through the pilot's window, which would be open during flight. We had our intercom set operating so that I could let Paul know when to shovel the stuff out.

Soon after takeoff, it started raining but we decided to press on. We headed for the Mazoe NDB then turned on to a heading to take us over the Dombashawa and Chisawasha TTLs then started the clock to time the drop. When we started the drop, it was raining hard, and the rain came in through the open the window. Paul threw out piles of leaflets and the odd poster as we proceeded along the run. Everything was going to plan, and we were slowly getting rid of the paper but with the open window, we both soon got soaked and water was sloshing around the floor of the plane. I saw that the intercept angle from the radio beacon, BZ NDB approaching our agreed end of run angle. We reversed course and headed back towards the Mazoe NDB all the while tossing out leaflets.

After a while I noticed that the aircraft was becoming difficult to control in pitch and the elevator felt spongy. Paul shone a flashlight onto the tailplane and there was the reason. Many of the leaflets were piling up on the wet leading edge of the tail and was spoiling the airflow over the left elevator surface.

We continued, with Paul throwing out larger piles of literature. We had planned a clean-up area at a bush strip to the east of the Wingate Golf, which lies in the northeastern area of Salisbury where a Field Reserve stick would set up a flare path and help clean up the plane.

I decided to call off the exercise after Paul had most of the stuff out because the plane was decidedly sluggish at the speed we were flying, which was about 110 knots. Initiating a climb or descent caused the plane to want to continue rotating.

We called up the Field Reserve stick and asked them to light up the flare path. Answer came back that they were having difficulty finding the airstrip and had not yet arrived. We hung around while the stick on the ground eventually found some vehicle tracks to the airfield. We could see the lights of their Land Rover heading in the right direction.

They laid out some goose necked flares alongside the runway and we landed. The pile of wet posters stuck to the right tailplane must have been four inches high.

We cleaned off any incriminating evidence as to what we had been up to that evening. However, some days later Dickie Dives, one of the DCA pilots from the Aerodromes Branch, presented me with a large envelope. I asked him what it was, and he just smiled. Inside the envelope was one of the documents that he had recovered from the rear of the plane!

John Munro[3]

For two years from 1974, I was in the BSA Police stationed at a small place called Binga halfway down the Lake Kariba. My first dealings with Pete Anderson, Copper 42, were in 1975 when he was available to assist anywhere on the lake but had based himself in Kariba town at the dam wall. Pete, a New Zealander, operated commercial flight charters using a Cessna 185 floatplane ZS-JKX out to the various tourist resorts and remote fishing lodges that dotted the shores of the lake. He was the natural go to person for search and rescue operations, which were mostly coordinated through the Lake Navigation Officer, nicknamed 'Gary Glitter', due to the gold insignia on his white uniform and white cap.

There were occasions when small fishing craft failed to report back to base, and Pete was called to conduct aerial searches, which were in the main successful. These tended to be infrequent due to the flying distance/time from Kariba to Binga area some 100km away. Pete was always very willing and keen to assist. I recall that Pete Anderson's co-pilot and floatplane assistant Peter Van Niekerk who was a Police Reservist and knew the Kariba Lake area well.

In 1977 while stationed at Bumi Hills, a post falling under Kariba itself, which I got to know Pete better and often flew lake short sorties with him along the Matusadona National Park boundary with the lake. We were mostly searching for illegal poaching and netting of fish as the area was very remote.

Bumi incorporated the extensive Omay Tribal Trust Land, normally accessed by mine proof vehicles or on foot patrols from the Siakobvu Base near the A1 road running parallel to the lake some 80 kilometres away from the shoreline between Karoi and Binga. The area was teaming with wild animals due to its proximity to the adjacent Matusadona National Park as well as a portion of the Chizarira National Park west of the Sengwa River.

Other Government services to the area included Internal Affairs as well as various military sectors. Within Internal Affairs, a Game Department section had been formed to perform duties related to the wellbeing and safekeeping of wildlife within the TTL. This group was headed by Dave Dunlop who hailed from a Kenyan wildlife organisation and was experienced in dealing with the work expected of him and his men.

On a hot summer`s afternoon the A60 radio base station adjacent to my office in the wooden office on the hill at Bumi cackled with the usual static prefacing a garbled message. The caller was Dave Dunlop who had been conducting a foot patrol with some of his men at the base of the Mapongolo Hills in the Omay TTL, 60 kilometres from the lake. He had come across a three-month-old elephant calf with a cable snare around its neck and had been abandoned by the herd.

The calf had been dragging a heavy Mopane log to which the cable snare had been attached with the result that the snare had imbedded itself deeply into the young elephant`s neck. Barely alive and so weak as to allow human interference without fuss, the young elephant had been released from the snare, but the wounds to her neck were serious. Struggling to walk, the baby elephant would be expected to die, or be savaged by hyenas, if not treated. Returning the calf to the dispersed herd would have been impossible and the location was so remote that vehicle recovery was out of the question. The only hope was to administer the best first aid and hope the herd would find the youngster. Shooting the animal and putting it out of its dilemma was debated as an option, but soon shelved.

I agreed with Dave that all attempts must be made to get medical aid to them to tend the elephant`s wound. I radioed Lake Navigation, and before long was linked to Pete Anderson. I explained the situation but also the dangers of flying 60 kilometres inland with a floatplane and no luxury of water to land the craft in the event of a problem. Pete had no hesitation in providing me his ETA at Katete Harbour to collect me with the necessary medical supplies we would drop to the ground team.

The first thing I had to do was to gather all the medical the supplies I could find. I raided the station first aid boxes and depleted them of all the cotton wool, crepe bandages, iodine, mercurochrome, and whatever padded gauzes there were. A quick trip down to the nearby Bumi Hills Safari Lodge resulted in bath towels, tables, clothes and hotel sheets torn into strips being stuffed into a 200lb grain bag along with antiseptic creams and other oddments. The result was an overstuffed hessian bag bulging at the seams and weighing in at about 20lbs of assorted medication.

Pete landed the red and white mercy machine in a short distance, manoeuvring between the dead Mopane trees jutting out of the water in the approach inlet and pulling up alongside the jetty. A quick briefing of the situation followed and a suitably folded 1:50,000 map of the Mapongolo area was scanned with keen eyes. Where was the nearest stretch of water for an emergency landing if required? Choices were few – Ume River or Sengwa River, both equidistant from the site of the stricken elephant at around 30km and then there was no guarantee of a clear landing spot. With limited leeway we took off heading inland away from the lake.

The hot gusts of air drafting upwards from the parched earth below resulted in some turbulence as we sped just above the dry, arid Omay TTL and its small groups of Batonka huts baking in the hot sun. We flew over Chief Mola`s area and in the distance could see the haze of the Mapongolo Hills, the other side of which lay the area under Chief Negande`s control. The bush thickened as we drew closer to the map reference location where we were headed and before long the hills were upon us.

I turned on the mobile A60 radio and it was not long before my calls were responded to, and I knew we were close to the group on the ground. Dave had made his way to the nearest rocky outcrop to gain a better signal and by descriptions given I observed the clear white back of his 1:50,000 map held up as a beacon against a fallen Baobab tree. Having made comms with the group and connected visually on the rocky outcrop, I instructed Pete to circle around and establish the lay of the surrounding ground, and locate the injured elephant. It took two turns before we saw three of Dave`s scouts standing alongside the small pachyderm beneath the minimal shade of a Combretum tree and Dave making his way down the rocky slope towards the beast.

Another conversation over the crackling radio informed Dave that on the next circle I would drop the overfilled grain bag from the aircraft at a point where we believed it would land safely close to where the elephant lay. Pete began his last turn lowering to about 60 feet above the treetops. He instructed me to open the plane door and manoeuvre the laden hessian bag onto the float pod beneath in preparation for the drop. I did this and, in the process, balanced myself half in the plane and the other half perched precariously on the pod balancing the 'medical package'. Pete called across to me indicating he would give the thumbs up when I should jettison the supplies. At a point, he pulled back on the throttle and the plane shuddered and shook as it dropped to just above the ever-nearing treetops. Looking ahead I could see the small group assembled on the ground and at what seemed to be at a snail`s pace in the air we approached the drop zone.

Out of the corner of my eye and whilst steadying myself with one leg on the pod outside the plane, I saw the thumbs up based on Pete`s calculations as to when the drop should take place. With

Pete Anderson in ZS-JKX departs Caribbea Bay resort, Kariba. On the left is a police patrol boat with the resort in the background (Photo by Peter Anderson)

a careful heave, I lifted and pushed the full hessian bag off the pod and watched as it plummeted earthwards destined to land in the small opening.

Unfortunately, this mercy mission missile was not to land as intended, as I saw one of Dave`s scouts rushing towards the open ground with his arms stretched skywards. I immediately realised what he was about to do but could do nothing to prevent it. Oblivious to the weight and speed of the oncoming parcel the scout braced himself with arms aloft. From above we witnessed a whirlwind of arms, legs, sack, sticks and dust – all at once. My lasting visions was one of a game scout tumbling head over heels through the Mopane scrub and down a rocky embankment closely followed by one hessian sack full of medical supplies. Others rushed to his aid but the damage had been done. We now had two casualties on the ground.

Calls to Dave via the A60 radio pronounced that the scout was suffering not only from the embarrassing mirth coming from his colleagues but had incurred several cuts and bruises to add to his now broken arm! Our duty done, there was not much more that we could do from the air so after an obligatory wiggle of the wings, Pete turned heading for the far distant lake.

We later heard from Dave and his team that despite our efforts in the mercy flight, the young elephant had succumbed to its injuries later in the day.

I left the Lake at the end of 1977, to return as the Officer in Charge at Kariba itself in May 1981. I remained there until July 1982, when I left the BSA Police and went farming. There was an occasion during my tenure as OiC Kariba that on a Friday afternoon the CAPCO [Central African Power Corporation] control room near the dam wall received a garbled message that a boat with five occupants had capsized on the Zambezi River near Mapata Gorge, near Kanyemba downstream from Kariba. The message was rather unclear, but we knew there had been an incident. Although outside of the Kariba Police District, I notified the Officer Commanding Lomagundi District and suggested that at first light on the Saturday morning I would proceed with Pete to conduct a recce along the river and establish what had transpired. At the time there was an American exploratory drilling team collecting soil samples for a proposed dam on the Zambezi at Mapata Gorge and I believed that the missing people may well have belonged to their group.

At 0500, I met Pete at the Caribbea Bay harbour, and we took off following a north-east heading, which was the most direct route to Kanyemba at the headwaters of Cabora Bassa Lake further downstream. Flying early morning in a floatplane over the Zambezi Valley and escarpment was an experience not to be forgotten. We flew high and into the rising sun, so game viewing was out of the question, but the magnificence of the area and its bush was superb. It was about an hour's flying time to Kanyemba. From there we backtracked upstream at low level to a recognised fishing camp near the American base. Here we landed on the flowing river and idled to the bank where we were met by a crowd of Batonka fishermen who proceeded to inform us that the previous evening when checking their fishing nets, two of their Makoro dugout canoes had been attacked and overturned by an irate hippo.

Once capsized, the Makoros floated away downstream and their occupants disappeared into the turbulent waters and were not seen again. At that point, the river flow speeds up as it narrows through the Mapata Gorge. We decided that the only action we could take was to fly down the river from the gorge, and look for stranded persons or bodies. We flew up to Kanyemba on both the Zambian bank and the Zimababwe bank. As hostilities between the two countries has ceased with Zimbabwean independence, we were safe to fly into Zambian airspace.

Our search covered over 20 kilometres of shoreline, but we found nothing. On the flight back, Pete flew at low level following the river. We saw a huge variety of game including lion, rhino, elephant, buffalo, hippo, crocodile, and all species of antelope. It had been an early start and an intense search. Pete selected a sandbank in the centre of the Zambezi, landed and eased the plane up to the sandbank. I leapt out and secured the pods with ropes before putting out the primus stove, kettle and sandwiches and making tea. The birdlife in the surrounding bush, the thrashing of tiger-fish in the water and the bellowing of a nearby herd of buffalo added to the tranquillity in which we enjoyed our breakfast in the morning sun.

After breakfast, we continued our low-level flight upstream. Passing Mana Pools with its magnificent tree line and national parks office, we stuck to the river route enjoying the scenery as we did so. On reaching Chirundu, Pete developed his mischievous grin and said, "Hold onto your seat." It was then I realised what he would be doing and the bridge linking the two countries loomed closer as he nosed downwards. We swooped under the road bridge skimming the water below with our pods and then headed for A Camp at the mouth of the Kariba Gorge. Low flying was still the order of the day when Pete entered the bottom of Kariba Gorge and deftly took the plane a further 20km before the curved dam wall loomed ahead and we rose for the occasion. Once we had landed outside Caribbea Bay and idled onto a mooring point, it struck home to me how privileged I had been at the expense of lives of the five men.

Bob Needham: Copper 33[4]

Twelve years into the bush war in Rhodesia. I'm in a hut at the JOC down at the far end of runway 17 at Fort Victoria airfield, Victoria Province. It was early on the morning of 23 October 1976, and it is unusually hot for this time of the year. I was having a bad night, tossing, and turning in my sleeping bag when someone battered on the door down and called out "Bob, get down to briefing pronto, something's going down." "Okay, Okay, I'll be there in a few minutes," I mumbled in return. I always slept fully clothed in my camouflage uniform whilst on operational duty, so getting to the briefing room took no time at all. A quick splash of water on my face in the ablutions block and I was ready to go.

The briefing room was dimly lit, hot and airless and the fan in the ceiling just made an annoying click, click, click sound as it stirred the hot smoky atmosphere around with absolutely no effect on its temperature at all. A few other unshaved personnel in bits and pieces of military undress were lolling around on chairs rubbing the sleep out of their eyes and waiting for the briefing to start. I assumed they had good reasons for being there since nobody in their right mind would put themselves through this agony for entertainment. Getting out my damp notebook and pencil, I wiped the sweat trickling into my eyes with the back of my hand and promptly nodded off to sleep only to be awoken by the briefing officer introducing himself.

I seem to remember his name was Denis Mahon, an American, ex-Vietnam War veteran now serving with the 2nd Btn Rhodesian African Rifles. The briefing was delivered in typical stilted military style. Short, sharp and to the point. At last light the evening before, 15 plus CTs had been sighted by an O.P. in the immediate Dove Dam area, 74 nautical miles east of Fort Victoria and just south of the Fort Victoria to Umtali road. Fire Force Delta, 2nd Battalion Rhodesian African Rifles were to be deployed.

The first wave of Fire Force Delta was to be airlifted into the Dove Dam area at dawn. Adopting standard tactics, the Fire Force was made up of twelve troops in three stop groups, each consisting of four men, one per G-car, led by the K-car carrying the Fire Force Commander. On arrival over the operational area the K-car would orbit at 800 feet above ground level while the Fire Force Commander assessed the situation and formulated his battle plan. The three stop groups will deplane as directed by him.

If no immediate contact with the enemy was made the stop groups, would sweep forward and adopt ambush positions. Lieutenant Mahon pointed out where the O.P. had sighted the CTs and possible G-car drop positions on the large briefing map on the wall but re-emphasised that the Fire Force Commander in the K-car would make the final decisions. He went on to explain that these operations tended to be very fluid and a decision made might well be changed by the commander five minutes later.

The whole operation seemed a little bit light on to, but it was a fact that the regular Rhodesian security forces had become stretched to the very limit by this time of the war. Only a couple of months back, in August, the South African Government had created huge gaps in our defence force by starting to withdraw its support for the Smith Government. This started with the withdrawal back to South Africa of 26 of its helicopters and 50 pilots and technicians that were on loan us.

Anyway, as I sat there listening to a brief that didn't seem to have anything much to do with me, I was starting to wonder where I came into all this. I was not left in doubt for long. As Lt Mahon continued with the brief it became obvious that the part time, Police Reserve Air Wing was going to be used more and more on hot operations to fill the gaps created by the South African Government withdrawal of support.

I heard Lieutenant Mahon say, "Task for Copper 33. Because of the broken countryside Copper 33 will position overhead the Dove Dam at 05.20 hours just before sunup to assist Fire Force Delta with Telstar relay communication operations as required. Aeroplane will be Piper Cherokee 260 VP-YKD. Air crew will be pilot R. Needham, British South Africa Police and radio operator Corporal. R. Van der Merwe, Rhodesian Air Force. Will those two-air crew stand up and identify themselves to each other?" I stood up at the same time as a 20 something-year-old, ginger haired, freckle-faced youth, stood up two seats away. We nodded at each other and sat down.

The grey flying suit used by Bob Needham sports a version of the Mat Prov flight patch, (issued to all of the flight towards the end), PRAW epaulettes and the pilot's name. The camouflage jacket has the B.S.A.P. insignia on the collar, the wire embroidered B.S.A.P. Reserve Airwing pilot's wings. Below the wings are the Rhodesia General Service and the Zimbabwe Independence medals, worn on special parades only. Placed on the jacket are two of the three types of shoulder patch worn on a uniform shirt, one for each of the reserve services in which Bob served. The blue Paisley scarf is Bob's 'lucky flying scarf' bought for his first flying lesson and worn on every PRAW operational flight. (Photo by Bob Needham)

Lieutenant Mahon continued the briefing in short sharp staccato sentences. "Fire Force Delta call signs may be sweeping towards other friendly stationary call signs waiting in ambush in broken country with every possibility of poor VHF communications. Great caution must be exercised to avoid a friendly fire situation. Full use of the Telstar relay facilities provided by Copper 33 will be used by all call signs if in any doubt. It is imperative that positions be passed in Shackle before the fire fight commences or any physical contact is made with the enemy."

A list of VHF radio frequencies, radio call signs and map references followed at the end of the briefing and finally the all-important 10 letter Shackle code word of the day was written down and committed to memory. As usual Mahon finished by asking for any questions.

It crossed my mind to ask why I was being tasked to conduct the Telstar relay communications for the operation. Surely, Fire Force Commander in the K-car would normally do this, as part of his duties wouldn't he?

As I raised my hand to ask the question the words from Lord Alfred Tennyson's famous poem 'The charge of the Light Brigade' sprang to mind. 'Theirs not to reason why, theirs but to do and die', plus I suddenly baulked at showing my ignorance to a whole room of professional soldiers and airmen so instead I blurted out, "Any intelligence on whether the CTs are carrying Strellas or not?" Heads turned and the silence seemed to last forever as Lieutenant Mahon pondered the question. Certainly, time enough for my guts to give a wrench and churn over. I felt sick. "No intelligence on that but in my opinion, they are probably not carrying SAM7s" was the reply. Thank God for that. Just small arms fire I thought as my stomach returned to its more normal slightly nauseated feeling that I always got before flying into a hot area.

A few birds were giving the odd chirp to welcome in the new day and the camp was beginning to stir as I made my lonely way in the dark to the all ranks mess. The only other person in the mess was the young Air Force Corporal who was to be my radio operator. Maybe I was getting cynical by this time of the war, but as we talked about the upcoming flight, I got the distinct impression that he had not done much of this sort of work before. At least he seemed to know how to operate the Shackle code and had the Shackle word of the day written on his signal pad in big letters. All he had to do was relay messages, probably in veiled talk, and pass grid reference positions in Shackle. Surely, that couldn't be that hard? I had done it on many Telstar operations in the past with PATU sticks and my usual PRAW observer/gunner did it all the time. However, I still could not shake a sense of foreboding as we walked out to the aeroplane tie down area where I started to conduct the pre flight inspection on our Cherokee 260 aeroplane, VP-YKD.

Thirty minutes later, lined up on the centre line of runway 17 and with a faint whisper of grey showing in the sky to the east on my left, I opened the throttle and roared down the runway into the black. I kept the landing and navigation lights off as I didn't want to advertise my departure to any CTs that might be lurking off the end of the runway with a Sam7 missile ready to shoot me down.

The navigation would be easy, just turn left at the end of the runway and follow the Umtali road that I could dimly see from 300 feet out of the cockpit window on my left.

It promised to be a fine day as the first rays of the sun started to spill out over the horizon and paint the cirro cumulus clouds high overhead in shades of gentle pearly pink. I had always loved that type of mackerel skyscape ever since I first became aware of it during my early days as a boy learning to fly on Tiger Moths, in the early morning mists of Croydon Airport in South London. I smiled and relaxed at the memory and my stomach settled down. I always felt better once I was airborne and in my familiar environment. I checked my watch and map, which confirmed that I was very close to the operational area. Down below the sun was still a tad below the horizon when suddenly it broke clear and the Dove Dam caught the first rays and flared brilliant silver. Yes, spot on time. Spot on position. As I went into a left-hand orbit at 2,000 feet above ground level the radio operator made a good clear radio contact with the Fire Force Commander in the K-car informing him in veiled talk that Copper 33 was in position.

Thereafter we maintained strict radio silence as I reduced power and airspeed, then reset the propeller pitch and the mixture to the recommended settings for endurance flying. Catching the odd glimpse of the K-car circling below me and saw the G-car helicopters parked in some contoured mealie fields nearby, no doubt re-briefing, it was apparent that the operation had already started but the only sound on the VHF radio was the usual static. My assumption was that contact with the CTs had not been made so far and that the Fire Force stops were sweeping ahead as briefed by Sunray.

That was exactly what was happening. One of those Fire Force soldiers was 21-year-old Private Julian Chinaka Tarusarira sweeping forward in line abreast together with the three other Rhodesian African Rifles soldiers of his stick. Private Tarusarira was a company signaller currently serving with 6 platoon, D Company, 2nd Battalion the Rhodesian African Rifles. He had been with the unit since its formation earlier in the year on 2 January 1976 and was known as a cheerful sort of a chap and popular with other members of his unit.

I don't know if he was the stick leader but he was certainly carrying either the A63 or A76 VHF radio normally carried by the stick leader. He also carried a Belgian FN self-loading rifle with 100 rounds of NATO 7.62 ammo in magazines with every third or fourth round a tracer. The sights of his rifle were set for 100 metres close combat and just like the others in the stick he was also carrying one M962 HE grenade, one M970 white phosphorus grenade, a smoke grenade and a couple of rifle grenades plus an Icarus flare. Again, just like the others, he carried a saline drip which he had been trained how to use and a lightweight sleeping bag plus the usual battle rations and water bottles.

Meanwhile the temperature in the cockpit of Copper 33 at 2,000 feet overhead was slowly creeping up and the engine oil temperature was a little on the high side too, but not in the red – yet. Cylinder head temperature looked good, but I knew that I would need to keep an eye on that oil temperature. Various other thoughts sprang into my mind. Perhaps it is going to be a lemon and I could get back to Fort Victoria for a more substantial breakfast and then back home to Bulawayo at the end of my ten-day tour. On the other hand, we could be orbiting for hours so I would need to monitor my fuel usage very closely.

I changed the fuel tank selector from the left tank to the right I and wrote the time for the next fuel tank change in the fuel log. The morning wore on and the situation remained unchanged apart from the cockpit temperature, which was by now very uncomfortable. I closed the outside air vents, which were operating like hair dryers. Both the radio operator and I were drinking copious quantities of water, but I knew that we would pay the penalty later. At least we would have empty water bottles by then. All in all, it was a pretty miserable flight crew sitting in a lather of sweat and orbiting the Dove Dam at 2,000 ft. on that October morning in 1976. Was it my imagination or was that engine oil temperature increasing? Looking around at the countryside below all I could see was small gomosand – very small, contoured mealie fields. Certainly not the best forced landing country in the world but better than nothing.

Back down on the ground I'm sure that Private Tarusarira was equally suffering from the heat with Mopani flies settling on his eyelids and lips as, no doubt dripping with sweat, he carried his heavy load of rifle, radio, ammo, and grenades through the bush and around the bald grey gomos. Heavy on his mind would have been the thought that he and the rest of his line abreast, spread-out Fire Force stop, would be very close to the Fire Force ambush stops by now. Communications with the K-car seemed to have dried up, so Private Tarusarira decided to pass his grid position in Shackle to us in Copper 33 circling overhead, and request that it be relayed, also in Shackle, over the operational frequency, thus alerting the Fire Force Delta stops waiting in ambush positions to hold fire if in any doubt of the identity of approaching personnel.

In the aeroplane, I was getting quite concerned about the oil temperature now and set the mixture full rich to cool it down. In the background, I was vaguely aware that my radio operator seemed to be having trouble with the Shackle but as I was concentrating on my engine overheating problems, I didn't help him out. Thirty seconds later and still worrying about the oil temperature that was increasing I felt that we might have to return to base shortly.

On the radio a highly agitated voice which was cut off in mid-sentence identifying the man as RAR. In the background during this transmission, I could hear very heavy automatic rifle fire. I drew in a sharp intake of breath as a sickening silence followed except for the radio gently hissing static. The radio operator and I looked at each other but couldn't find any words. Shortly thereafter, another voice called up the Fire Force Commander in the K-car below us and informed him that one of our soldiers had been killed by friendly fire. It turned out that Julian and his stick had walked into one of the Fire Force stops waiting in ambush for the CTs to pass through their area. The silence in the cockpit was palpable.

646091 Private Julian Chinaka Tarusarira, company signaller, 6 Platoon, D Company, 2nd Battalion Rhodesian African Rifles died instantly in a friendly fire incident at approximately 06.30 hours on the morning of 23 October 1976, and I thought that my radio operator and I had got the Shackle all wrong and were responsible. That is what I was thinking when the sound of silence in the cockpit became even more profound. The engine of good old reliable KD had failed on me. Bloody hell, just not my day; in the space of a minute, or so I thought, I had helped to kill one of our own soldiers and this was quickly followed by an engine failure over an area where a CT firefight was just about to ramp up.

A moment of painful shock sliced through my chest. Breathing heavily, my training kicked in and without thinking, I selected the attitude for best glide-speed with the elevators and trimmed the aeroplane to fly hands off. At the same time, I found myself automatically turning away from what I now thought was an active terrorist contact area and happily heading away from the only half-decent, forced landing field within gliding distance.

I always had a deep fear of being captured and tortured by terrorists so the fact that I was headed away from a possible forced landing area but also a possible contact area and toward some large gomos to the North-West didn't seem to faze me too much as I went through my restart drills. Throttle set, mixture rich, fuel pump on, fuel selector to fullest tank. There it was, staring me in the face. What a bloody idiot. I had run a fuel tank dry. I quickly changed tanks and, seconds later, the engine roared into life again. I couldn't believe that I had committed such a stupid basic mistake. A short while later, as we climbed back up, Sunray came up on the radio from the K-car and informed all units that the operation was called off and that Copper 33 was released to return to base.

I levelled off at 2,000 feet and resumed my normal, fast cruise speed and, as expected, the oil temperature needle now fell back to its normal comforting position on the gauge. No engine overheating problem at all. My radio operator and I flew back down the Fort Victoria road to the airfield in miserable silence, still thinking that we might have caused the death of one of our own. I will always remember how various Rhodesian African Rifles call signs occasionally called us up to enquire if we knew the name of the soldier who had been killed and I couldn't help but sense that this then unnamed, dead African soldier was part of a very large close knit warrior family.

A few weeks later I heard that we had not made a mistake on the Shackle relay and the accident had happened for other reasons.[5]

B.S.A.P. PRAW Training Day Mikado Farm Matprov

It was decided to have a training day at Mikado Farm, Robin Watson's place near Bulawayo. The idea was for the Bulawayo PRAW pilots and observers to get in some air to ground firing practice with the .303 Browning machine gun. While a 45-gallon drum target was being set up in one of the farm dams, and Dave Owen our regular B.S.A.P. P.O. armourer was setting up the gun in Pat Wesson's Cherokee 6, Robin suggested that while we waited the two of us fly together in his V-tailed Bonanza. It was also an opportunity for me to conduct his annual PRAW check flight, which was about due. I

Two members of the Bulawayo Flight sheltering from the sun under the wing of Robin Watson's Bonanza, during a break in the training at Mikado Farm. Visible is the starboard .303. Browning machine gun and housing. (Photo by Bob Needham)

VP-WHM at speed over the dry African veldt showing a clear view of the gun pods (Photo by Hugh Bomford)

ZS-IWW a Cessna P206D seen here at a PRAW training day held on Robin Watson's Mikado Farm. It is fitted with an undercarriage mounted, bomb rack, the release cable can be seen running into the cabin, and a .303 machine gun mounted at the open rear doorway. (Photo by Bob Needham)

jumped at the chance, as I was rather keen to see how the aeroplane's twin underslung machine guns affected its performance.

We were quickly aloft and the first thing I called for on the test was for Robin to demonstrate a basic stall and a standard recovery. Off came the power the nose was gently raised, and we approached the stall. So far so good. Then about five knots before the stall and with the stall warning going off, I heard a 'rumble, rumble' sound followed by a sharp metallic 'clunk' at the point of stall. Then as Robin demonstrated a very sound minimum height loss recovery by quickly lowering the nose and applying full power, I distinctly heard the same 'rumble, rumble clunk' sound again. Although I knew Robin had checked for loose objects and secure a bag in the back before commencing the flight clearly there was something loose floating about in the aeroplane. On pointing this out to Robin he nonchalantly replied, "Oh that will be my bag of hand grenades in the back that has come loose again. Just hop in the back and grab the bag and I'll show you how it works." As you can imagine, I was in the back in a blur, grabbed the bag of hand grenades and was strapped back in the front in a trice. At the same time, I politely declined his offer of a grenade launch demonstration, mumbling something about running late with the training exercise. I finished

Mike Gard, Bulawayo Flight Commander at the time of the training day on Robin Watson's Mikado Farm, looking at the two 15kg fragmentation bombs mounted on the port undercarriage leg of Colin Bickle's Cessna 206 Turbo Stationair VP-WIL. (Photo by Bob Needham)

up Robin's check ride with a couple of max rate turns, a simulated forced landing, and some very hairy low-level contour flying as only an ex-WW2 ground attack fighter pilot can do it. All this being done with me tightly clutching a bag of four hand grenades to my chest.

The day wore on and finally it was my turn to have a go at "the gun." Great fun. We flew in circles round the dam, and I used the bullet splashes in the water like tracer to walk the rounds up to the target. Now Rhodesian DRP camo trousers used to have button flies and one of my buttons was missing. You could say that it was an open invitation and, sure enough, after blasting away at the target for some minutes a red-hot doppie flew through the opening and lodged itself in my groin. I caught a glimpse of Pat Wesson, who was flying the aeroplane, looking at me over his shoulder in disbelief as I suddenly stopped firing the gun, frantically pulled my trousers down and started clutching at my groin like I had suddenly taken leave of my senses; all the while swearing my head off.

Next on the agenda was a ground attack demonstration by Robin in his Bonanza. Targets were set up in the stubble of a mealie field close to where we were all standing. Robin did a couple of low passes and, as expected, blasted the crap out of the target with his .303 machine guns. He then set up for a third pass and as he dived, we were close enough to see the grenade leave the aeroplane from where we stood. The explosion was not as loud as I would have expected, but just afterwards, a swarm of angry bees flew over our heads. As Robin positioned for a second grenade drop reality started to set in for the group. For as the second grenade exploded everyone was ready for a second swarm of bees and as I looked around, I saw that I was not the only one in the crouched position.

The Story Behind Alan Winter's Picture

Sometime in 1979–1980, I was briefed for a casevac mission to land on a particular dirt road in a terrorist-overrun area where a forward casualty clearing area had been set up close to an ongoing contact. The mission was to pick up casualties from the contact and fly them to the Bulawayo-Kumalo airfield. The contact involved a Rhodesian African Rifles Fire Force and an unknown number of terrorists. I was informed that the contact could still be in progress on my arrival and to be especially vigilant for Rhodesian Air Force Lynx aeroplanes putting in ground attacks in the area, as well as the usual Alouette G-car helicopters going about their business. I was concerned about the aeroplane's weight apropos of the take off distance available and the surface of the dirt road. No one could

Stinson 108-3 Voyager wearing the registration VP-WCV was built in 1947, and imported to South Africa as ZS-DEV. It was used by The New Zealand Churches of Christ to survey for missions in Northern and Southern Rhodesia. Purchased as VP-WCV by RPR Peter Scales, she was used on PRAW duties until June 1975, when exported to South Africa. It is still airworthy as ZS-JKV. (Artwork by Leon Manoucherians)

After the war, the Bonanza VP-YGZ was re-registered as Z-YGZ. It was in this scheme, with Rally Number B1, that it took part in and completed the World Vintage Air Rally from London to Sydney, in 1990. Bill Andrews and Jim Trounsen flew it to London from Zimbabwe for the start. At one stage, in Malaysia, Bill Andrews organised car fuel for competitors, when they landed and found no aviation fuel available. They finished the rally earning the Points Prize. (Artwork by Leon Manoucherians)

The Cessna 177 Cardinal VP-WEE was flown extensively by PRP Alan Murray, Copper 161. Of aircraft used for casualty evacuation, it was one that received hits from ground fire: one of bullets damaged the port wing attachment. (Artwork by Leon Manoucherians)

This Piper PA-23 Aztec of the Techair was based at Charles Prince Airport, and operated by John and Sylvia Plant. John was a PRP and often rented the company's aircraft to other PRAW pilots. Their proximity to the capital and link to PRAW meant that Techair was often the first to be approached to assist the B.S.A.P.. The aircraft was fitted with non-fuel-injected engines with an output of 250 horse power. Pilots that flew it often carried automatic weapons to guard it while landing on remote strips. (Artwork by Leon Manoucherians)

Cessna 206s were a popular choice of aircraft between PRAW pilots. They had a useful carrying capacity and the cabin was spacious enough to comfortably accommodate a gunner on the rear seats, and machine gun firing out of the rear door. This U.206F, registration ZS-IYN, was owned by Skyline Charters, and was sometimes fitted with a grenade launcher in the cargo pod, in addition to the machine gun. (Artwork by Leon Manoucherians)

The Bonanza F.35 registered as VP-WHM was one of best-known aircraft of the PRAW, because of its unusual under-wing machine gun installation, and a grenade tube in the cockpit. From 1975, it was owned by J. Robin Watson of West Nicholson. In 1983, it was de-militarised and re-registered as Z-WHM, and then sold to South Africa as ZS-SMF. Eventually, it was exported to the USA: during the shipping there, the container containing it was dropped and the aircraft damaged beyond repair. The fuselage was on sale for a while, but then reported as scrapped. (Artwork by Leon Manoucherians)

This Cessna 180H Skywagon was imported to Rhodesia by the Mission Aviation Fellowship. Following a minor accident and repair in 1978, it was purchased by Chris Thorne of the Mazoe Flight, PRAW. Because of the danger of man-portable air defence systems like Soviet-made 9K32M Strela-2 ('SA-7 Grail'), it was sprayed overall in 'anti-Strela' grey. Moreover, it was armed with a Browning machine gun. It was re-registered as Z-WMR in 1980. (Artwork by Leon Manoucherians)

This Cessna U.206 was acquired by the Matabeleland Flying School, and often flown by PRP Bob Needham. In February 1980, it was sold to Coley Hall Transport. (Artwork by Leon Manoucherians)

The Cessna 337C Super Skymaster served with Malawi Railways until 1974, when it was acquired by the District Development Fund in Rhodesia. It was a latecomer to PRAW duties when purchased by PRP L Engels, in late 1979. (Artwork by Leon Manoucherians)

Following elections of 1980, the Cessna U.206F registered as ZS-IYN – a veteran of long service with the PRAW, and numerous ground attacks – was re-painted in bright civilian colours. Re-registered as Z-WNK, it was exported in 1984. (Artwork by Leon Manoucherians)

Brian van Buuren's Cessna T.210 registered as ZS-JUM, and painted in overall anti-Strela grey, was re-registered as Z-BVR in 1980. The aircraft continued serving with the Zimbabwe Republic Police as a part of the Police Air Wing until some time in 1982. (Artwork by Leon Manoucherians)

The Cessna T.210 with registration Z-YLT, was used for 'rainmaking' with help of a hole in the fuselage through which nitrate crystals were fired into heavy clouds. Ian Steel, who was called up towards the end of the PRAW, flew it for a week at a time, for up to 35 hours. The aircraft continued serving as Z-YLT, while Ian Steel served as police pilot in the Zimbabwe Republic Police until 1984. (Artwork by Leon Manoucherians)

Pilot Olly Knight and Observer Peter Hart of the Matabeleland Police Reserve Air Wing were featured on the February 1973 cover of *The Outpost* when they refuelled their aircraft after an early morning mission over Northern Mashona land. (*The Outpost Magazine*)

Farmers from Centenary East/Mount Darwin serving in the Police Reserve Air Wing at the height of its military activities in 1979. From left: PRO Harvey Middleton, PRP Wally Barton. PRO Hennie Jooste, and PRO Ben Nieuwoudt. (*The Outpost Magazine*)

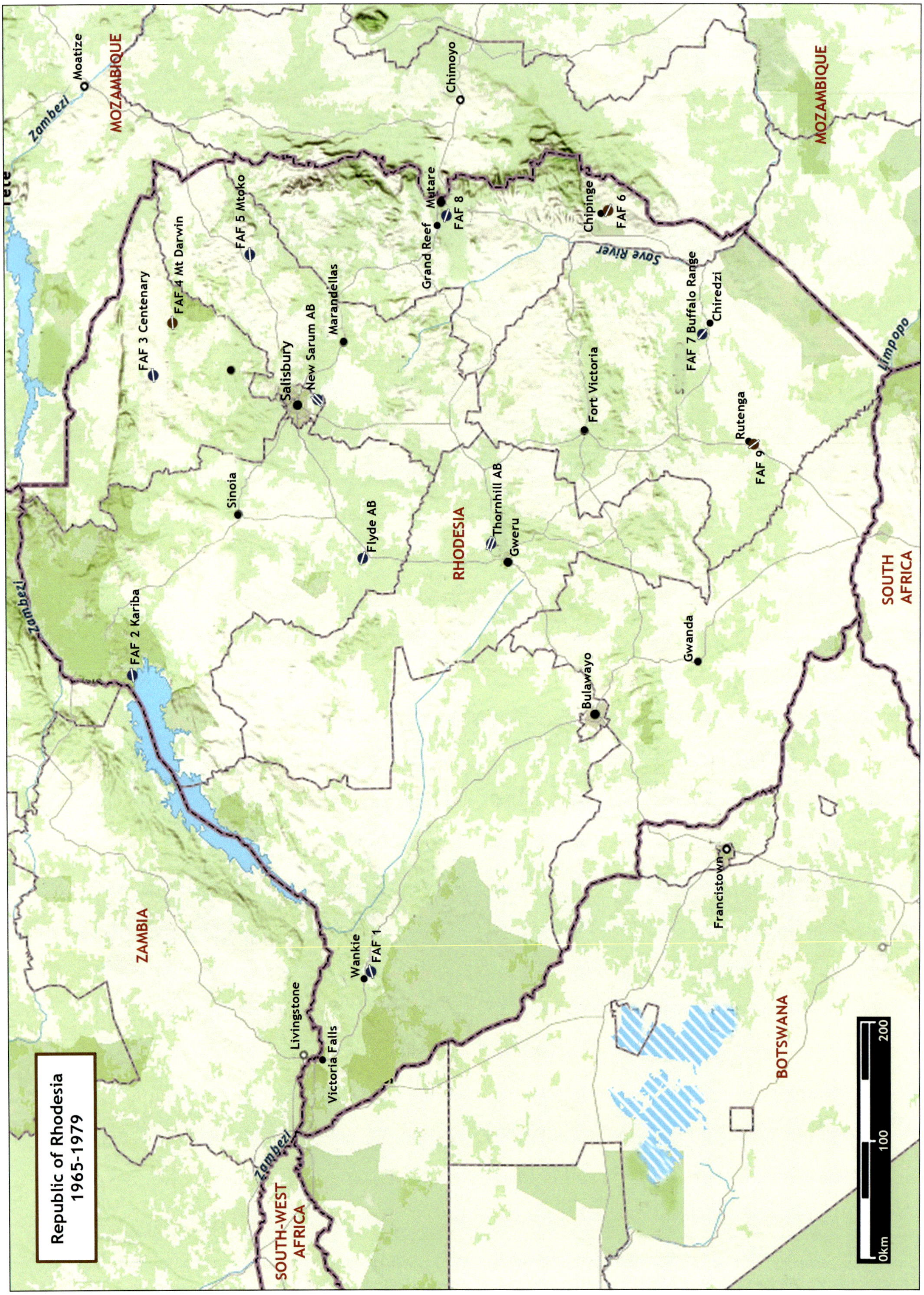
Republic of Rhodesia
1965-1979
MOZAMBIQUE
Moatize
Zambezi
Tete
Chimoyo
MOZAMBIQUE
FAF 3 Centenary
FAF 4 Mt Darwin
FAF 5 Mtoko
Mutare
FAF 8
Grand Reef
Chipinge
FAF 6
Save River
FAF 7 Buffalo Range
Chiredzi
Limpopo
Marandellas
New Sarum AB
Salisbury
Fort Victoria
Rutenga
FAF 9
Sinoia
Flyde AB
Thornhill AB
Gweru
RHODESIA
Zambezi
FAF 2 Kariba
Gwanda
SOUTH AFRICA
Bulawayo
Francistown
ZAMBIA
Wankie
FAF 1
Livingstone
Victoria Falls
BOTSWANA
Zambezi
SOUTH-WEST AFRICA
0km
100
200

ZS GBL taking off from a dirt road in a hot contact area with a casualty. This picture was painted by Alan Winter, Bob Needham's observer of the incident described in 'The story behind Alan Winter's Picture.' (Art by Alan Winter)

The Matabeleland Flight devised this unofficial uniform patch. (Photo by Markham Batstone)

come up with answers, so I decided to leave behind my observer, Alan Winter.

At the time, my aeroplane was fitted with an armour-plated seat, which was strapped on top of the normal aeroplane seat. I had also been issued with a Rhodesian made flak jacket. The seat was wobbly, and extremely uncomfortable. The flak jacket was ill fitting, restrictive and very hot. I hated both. Because of my concerns about weight, and to maximise my casualty uplift capability I decided to ditch the armour-plated seat. In lieu of the protection from ground fire to the family jewels afforded by the heavy armoured seat, I placed my flak jacket on the floor just in front of the normal seat. I also removed the passenger doors, not forgetting to tape down the flap lowering safety switch in the doorjamb.

After landing on the dirt road, I joined a queue of aeroplanes behind a 4 Squadron Lynx and a Britain Norman Islander twin. I believe that the Lynx had just been putting in front gun and SNEB rocket attacks against the terrorists and was now being used in a Casavac role. A medic appeared as I closed the aeroplane down and asked if I could take a stretcher case and a medic. I answered in the affirmative and, having eyeballed the makeshift airstrip, said that I could also take one walking wounded casualty as well. The stretcher case turned out to be a black Rhodesian soldier and the walking wounded was a white Rhodesian officer, both of the Rhodesian African Rifles. The medic was a Rhodesian Indian Combat Medic. There was a slight delay loading the stretcher case as the soldier was still being stabilised while lying on his stretcher by the side of the road. As I waited, an officer advised me to be on the alert for G-cars flying in the area and deploying stop groups nearby, as the contact appeared to be moving in our direction. Sure enough, there was a G-car hovering just off the edge of the road, as I got airborne.

On the way back to Kumalo airfield it was getting dark, and the weather began to deteriorate. I started to fly in and out of cloud but at least that made the possibility of a SAM 7 Strella hit on the aeroplane remote. However, in the turbulence, while attempting to steady the drip the medic accidently grabbed the drip tube and pulled the drip right out of the RAR soldier's arm. The medic, who later admitted that this was his first solo airborne Casavac mission, started to panic as he struggled to find a vein in which to reposition the drip. The soldier's veins began to collapse as he started to go into shock. It became obvious that there was a real chance of losing him. We were all of us trained to put in drips but there was nothing I could do to help the medic and still fly the aeroplane in the deteriorating weather. Just then the RAR officer crawled painfully forward and managed to slap up a vein while the medic repositioned the drip. Thankfully the soldier started to stabilise once more.

I will never forget that scene as I looked over my shoulder. It is indelibly etched in my mind, and I can see it now as clearly today as I saw it then, over 40 years ago. Clouds, cold rain, and mist flashing past the open-door space in the dusk with seat belts sucked out and noisily hammering on the outside of the aeroplane. In rough turbulence and in the darkening gloom of the passenger space a heavily blood stained and bandaged white RAR officer and a Rhodesian Indian Combat Medic, both crouching over a black RAR soldier trying to reposition the drip and desperately fighting to save his life.

On return, I recounted the details of the flight to my observer/gunner, Alan Winter. He was an accomplished artist had been a RAF De Havilland Mosquito fighter-bomber pilot during WW2. A while later he presented me with the picture, which I have treasured ever since.

Flying from Induna

My wife Phoebe Ann did not fly for PRAW but was a fully qualified pilot and would fly mechanics and other passengers, as well as the aircraft used to drop sport parachutists. She would stay out at Nduna airfield after dark, occasionally on her own, waiting for me to return from B.S.A.P. operational flights. She would shine the car headlights across the threshold for me to see the start of the runway. The airfield was right next to a Tribal Trust Land and we gave up putting out a flare path because the people from the TTL used to steal the hurricane lamps when we were coming in for a landing. Later that TTL provide a base for a significant group of terrorists.

Phoebe Ann would drive out to the far end of the strip in our trusty Peugeot 404 station wagon. Three kids in the back and her Uzi submachine gun on her lap, safety catch off and ready for action. We had trained the children to reload the 25 round 9mm Uzi magazine and briefed them on immediate actions in the event of a terrorist attack.

After landing Phoebe Ann would follow me down the strip lighting the way with the car headlights to the tie-down area where I would quickly get out and if no one was in the Flying School, secure the aeroplane, hop into the car, and high tail it back to the relative safety of Bulawayo.

For a short while, the local Joint Operational Command positioned troops at the aerodrome who dug sandbagged trenches around the Flying School in anticipation of a possible terrorist attack. We also had a Fire Force equipped with Alouette Helicopters and Cessna Lynx aeroplanes based on the aerodrome at one point.

The Flying School was kitted out with Agric Alert, used by most farms and remote businesses. In the event of an attack, you pressed the button, and you were connected straight to the Joint Operational Command switchboard. It was better than nothing but depending on how far out you were in the sticks, reaction times could be a little slow. In our case, we were told that we would have to hold out for 45 minutes. Quite daunting for a husband and wife to be in a firefight, possibly on their own, and with the kids reloading the magazines. Luckily it never happened.

John Tayler: Copper 96[6]

I started flying in 1973 at the age of 33. Six of my fellow cotton farmers banded together to pay for an instructor and obtain their licences on a Piper Colt. I soloed after 20 hours and required another 30 hours to qualify. Three of us novice pilots decided to purchase and aircraft and selected to buy a 1966 Mooney M20C Mark 21 c/n 3360 ZS-EDM. This was 4-seater low wing aircraft with retractable undercarriage and very reliable and economical 180hp Lycoming 0-360-A1D180 HP engine. It was bought in 1973, from South Africa by Dr Burrows. An instructor, Mr Woodward, put us through some rigorous training. I eventually bought out my partners and normally flew the Mooney on PRAW flights. In about 1977, I had the underside of the wings painted with anti-Strella matt grey paint.

The aircraft came with Positive Control (PC), a factory fitted automated wing leveller, which was useful when multi-tasking in the cockpit. After about 15 years, the rubber bellows in the wings failed and I never had it fixed. It was fitted with manually actuated landing gear, with no hydraulics and electrics to go wrong. It was raised and lowered with a lever known as the Johnson Bar, which came up as fast as you could unlock the bar from just below the throttle and move it through 90 degrees and locking it in place on the floor. If an airstrip was short, and most were dirt, I would pull it off the ground and immediately lift the wheels, build up some speed and then pull up to get it over the trees at the end of the runway. Looked like cowboying but it worked. My wife Dot had also qualified on the Piper Colt, but when she came to convert to the Mooney, she was told women could not manage the manual undercarriage. She proved them wrong on the first attempt and has 400 hours on type.

The hydraulic flaps were brilliant and if coming in a bit fast and had a floater, the flaps could be released and they would retract slowly and at the same time you pulled back to compensate, which landed you in time to avoid excessive braking, as the Mooney also had small brake pads so you did not want to brake too hard as they would fade/heat up and not work too well. I once landed at a short bush grass strip and the grass had just been cut and was wet. Well, the brakes were useless, and I was aquaplaning, but I managed to ease the aircraft to the left of the runway and at the last minute put full right rudder, did a 180 and revved it a bit as still sliding backwards, and stopped in time.

It was a great plane, I used to load it with my wife, three small kids and camping stuff and fly to Mozambique's Bazaruto island on one tank, about 2.5 hours flying time, and land on a sand/grass strip, and after 2 weeks fly back on the other tank and land with about 15 minutes flying time back. It burnt 32 litres an hour and always blocked out at exactly 120kts.

John Tayler and his wife Dot who also flew the Mooney M20C ZS-EDM seen here at Christmas 2013, about the time the aircraft was sold and when John was 73 years old. Although concerned he would 'forget to put the wheels down one day' the main driver for the sale of EDM then Z-WNX was that after 36 years of farming at Mkwasine he was evicted in 2007. Like many in PAW, he could no longer justify or afford to keep the Mooney. (Photo by John Tayler)

If the runway was long enough, it could handle about 10 percent over weight. We lived in the low veldt at 1,500ft, which helped. I had an 800 metre, one way strip outside the back door of our sugar farm at Mkwasine, which meant only 1.5 hours flying time to the capital compared to a five-hour car trip.

It had a very small cabin area and could just squeeze three adult passengers. One evening whilst based at Buffalo Range I was tasked to fly to Chisumbanje, which was about 20 minutes flying time due east, to collect two badly

Seen at Chipinga airfield in 1978 is Cessna 172 VP-YYT, imported in 1965 by Cooper 72, Oliver Knight and Copper 74 John Hart, both members of the Matabeleland Flight. In the background is a Reims FTB337G Lynx being refuelled. (Brian Lambert)

Cessna 310P was operated from 1970 to 1986 by Cane Air in Rhodesia/Zimbabwe as ZS-IFD, and later registered as Z-WPS. Known to have been flown on PRAW duties by Cooper 165 Peter Wilson and others with SALOPS Flight and PGHQ Flight. It is seen here at Chipinga airfield in 1978. (Brian Lambert)

injured RAR guys who had been in a landmine blast. I landed in the dark with some flares to show me the strip and there were the guys on stretchers, hooked up to drips. There was no way I could get a stretcher in, so I told them if they wanted to get to hospital, they better get off the stretchers and crawl up onto the wing and into the back seats which they duly managed to do, and we hung the drips from the roof with less than half a metre elevation. They survived the trip, were stabilised at Chiredzi Hospital and the next morning I flew them to Salisbury, with a nurse in attendance kneeling on the front seat facing backwards to look after her patients. I did have a casevac flight to pick up a tracker dog that had been shot and wounded in the Mateke Hills in the far southeastern area of Rhodesia.

One night when flying to Harare with the family, the kids saw some shooting stars around the Gutu area. The only problem was that they were coming up from below us. Thankfully, we were high enough to avoid the tracer.

An unusual task I had was to deliver an oil filter to a Bedford RL troop carrier that was going to Renco Mine. They wanted me to drop the carefully wrapped parcel to them. The only problem being that it was not possible to open the door of a Mooney in flight and the part of the pilot's window that opened was too small for the parcel. I ended up landing on the main road and handing it to the driver.

We carried out a lot of convoy escorts from Triangle to Ngundu and from Masvingo to Beit Bridge. These flights were typically flown at 200 feet, and had a duration of about five hours. On one of the trips from Triangle, I was not popular with the convoy commander. My wife was in the convoy when our car had a puncture, and the spare was also flat, so there was much muttering whilst a vehicle rushed back to Triangle to get it repaired whilst I remained as top cover.

On the Beit Bridge trips, we used to land on the road outside the *Lion and Elephant* Motel and park in their lay-by and wave at the passing convoy as it pulled in for a leg stretch and shake.

On another occasion I took an Air Force Volunteer Reserve from FAF7 (Buffalo Range) with me as observer, and after flying for many hours above the convoy I buzzed the Mazda escort at the back of the convoy to say good bye as it entered Beit Bridge, and unbeknownst to me this was exactly where there was some rising ground with an extended high telephone line crossing the road which we proceeded to fly under and cut the wires with the tail. Luckily, only minor skin damage and we landed safely – lesson learnt!

One day when flying my neighbour, Alistair Davies's Cherokee 6 PA 32-300, VP-WFV, from Buffalo Range to Perrims in Mutare with a highly decorated senior Selous Scout, I was about to change fuel tanks (there were four to manage) when I was told over the radio to look out for some Hunters flying in the area. I looked down and there were four, I think, flying underneath us on their way to Mozambique so I pointed them out to my passenger whereupon my engine cut out. Well, after changing tanks, the engine woke up and I looked across to a very white-faced and angry scout who would

G.P. & S. 79951.

GENERAL CONVOY INSTRUCTIONS

General

1. These instructions are issued for the benefit of all persons who travel in the convoy. Please make sure that all your passengers are aware of these instructions and comply with them.

2. Before the convoy departs ensure that you have sufficient fuel, that your vehicle tyres are correctly inflated and you have a spare wheel and jack in case of punctures.

3. Attendance in the convoy is voluntary. However, once you join the convoy you come under the command and control of the convoy commander.

Road rules

4. Whilst on the road the normal rules of the road will apply and they must be observed.

Spacing

5. The spacing between vehicles should be 100 metres behind any escort vehicle and 50 metres between other vehicles. Large gaps are to be avoided.

Escort vehicles

6. There will be three escort vehicles; one at the head of the convoy, one approximately in the centre and the third at the rear. All these vehicles are in radio contact with each other as well as with other patrol vehicles on the road.

Breakdowns

7. Should any vehicle break down, it must pull off to the left of the road and assistance will be given by one of the escort vehicles, or by one of the other patrol vehicles on the road.

Air cover

8. If aeroplanes are heard or seen overhead, do not worry as from time to time we provide air cover for convoys as well.

Animals

9. You are likely to meet game and also cattle on the road, so be prepared for them.

Nature's calls

10. So that the convoys are not unduly delayed, please make sure that all calls of nature are attended to before the convoy sets off.

Overtaking

11. Whilst driving please do not overtake or attempt to jump the queue. We have enough to deal with without having to investigate road accidents on the way.

Medical

12. In the event of an accident or attack which necessitates medical attention, casevac will be arranged by the quickest means available.

Briefing

13. Fifteen minutes before the convoy sets off, a briefing will be held at the centre escort vehicle. The signal to attend will be the sounding of the hooter of the centre escort vehicle. At this briefing you will be instructed as to what action to take in the event of an attack.

Personal weapons

14. If you have personal weapons remember that they are for your personal protection. Please handle them carefully with due regard for the other members of the convoy. Personal weapons must be "made safe" just before you arrive at your convoy destination.

At destination

15. Once you have completed your journey with the convoy, please hand in these instructions to the Police in charge of your convoy. If you forget to do this please destroy this document as the detail it contains may be of some interest to our enemies.

Thank you. We hope you have a pleasant journey.

Each convoy was strictly managed along the rules listed here. When air cover was provided (Point 8), it was mostly by PRAW aircraft. (Bill Linfield Collection)

After the consortium Brian van Buuren was in sold their Piper Tri-Pacer VP-YLE he purchased a Cessna 210 Turbo Centurion ZS-JUM. This was never armed but was used on two occasions to deploy hand dropped, custom made bombs. Post 1980 the registration was changed to Z-BVB, and it is in this guise that it is seen at speed at low level. (Brain van Buuren)

not talk to me again, and his medals were definitely for ground operations.

And finally. When flying Clive and Rod Styles Cessna 182 VP-WCL out of an airstrip next to the railway line to Mozambique a few kilometres from the border at Malvernia/Sango, known as Boli International, after dark, and towards a storm over the border with no ground lights at all, I turned left sharply and low. I was looking for the lights of Chiredzi on the horizon and saw nothing as the unfamiliar high wing was blocking the view, and then the stall warning went off. Thankfully, the Cessna was very forgiving as I forced myself to level off and fly towards the storm and then slowly turn.

I ended up with 3,300 hours mostly in the Mooney with about 3,700 landings as most PRAW flights were around 30 minutes. ZS-EDM became Z-WNX in February 1985. I stopped flying in 2013 at 73 years of age and sold the Mooney, which is now based in Mutare. Age was a factor but mainly it was an economic decision after being removed off the land after 36 years of farming at Mkwasine in 2007.

Officer of the Legion of Merit for distinguished service to Rhodesia. This is the Civilian Division of the medal. (Paul Brewster)

Rhodesia General Service Medal (GSM) – for service on operations undertaken for the purpose of combating terrorist or enemy incursions into Rhodesia. Recipients had to have served in a military role for at least 91 days or have complete 14 days operational service, or engaged in active combat, or were in close contact with terrorists or the enemy. (Paul Brewster)

Rhodesia Meritorious Conduct Medal (MCM) – for brave and gallant conduct over and above the call of duty in a non-combatant capacity. This was awarded to civilian and service personnel of the RSF. (Paul Brewster)

Police Reserve Long Service Medal – for long and exemplary service. Award after nine years voluntary service in the BSAP 'A' Reserve or 15 years in the Field Reserve. (Paul Brewster)

Appendix I
Nominal Roll

Complied by Wayne Kennerley, based on the work of Peter and Anne Cooke, with updates from Guy Ellis

Copper No	Surname	Name	Initials	Force No	Pilot/Obs	Flight	Registration	Aircraft	Notes
168	Abrey	Alan	A. N. S.	21988Z	PRP	PGHQ Sby	ZS-JIL	Cherokee 6	A veterinarian later lived in Natal, South Africa. Formed the Umgeni Bird Park.
	Adams	John Peter	J. P.	3812S	PRO				
169	Addison	Alan	A. C.	22589C	PRP	SALOPS Recce Flight; PGHQ Sby			Operational call sign ALPHA 7, also Copper 231 PGHQ Flight PR 45/L/2, 287 SALOPS Flight
175	Addison	Dave	D. C.	14374Y	PRP	PGHQ Sby			
51	Aitken	James	J. W.	10097Z	PRP	Manicaland Flight, Mazoe Valley Flight 1970	VP-YRV	PA-20-135 Pacer	Kirsty Chatham his daughter reports Copper 6 and 52, also Copper 58 and call sign CHEETAH 2 with Manicaland Flight C180 VP-WGU; Browning 303 on the seat rails with Kevin Ewart. Piper Pacer VP-YRV Mazoe Valley Flight Outpost Dec 67, p23 (photo). After the loss of his farm in Chiponga he moved to Scotland where he died in 2014
09	Alford	Tony Michael	A. M.	3626Q	PRP	Mazoe Valley Flight	VP-WDJ	Cessna 182K	An Accountant, Outpost Feb '78, p7 (photo)
	Anderle		W. L.	18347	PRO	Manicaland Flight			
151	Anderson	Roy Leslie	R. L.	15099L	PRP	PGHQ Sby	VP-YRS(2) - Also ZS-FVL; VP-WEL	PA-32-260 Cherokee	A sheep farmer, who's wife Shelagh was also a PRAW pilot. Flight Commander PGHQ Flight after Don Holland. (Copper 220?) - Outpost Apr '79, p.29, July '79, p.23.
165	Anderson	Shelagh, Mrs	S. M.	203886P	PRP	PGHQ Sby			First (and possibly only) Operational Woman PRAW Pilot, also first Rhodesian Woman racing driver, drove a Simca Aronde in the first Rhodesian Grand Prix, first Rhodesian member of the Ninety-Nines, a women pilots association. Wife of PRP Roy Anderson. Shelagh died in 2021

Copper No	Surname	Name	Initials	Force No	Pilot/Obs	Flight	Registration	Aircraft	Notes (*continued*)
42	Anderson	Peter	P. W.	24050Q	PRP	Lomagundi Flight	ZS-JKX	Cessna 185 Floatplane	Operated a float plane on Kariba for tourists and businesses on the lake
283	Anderson	Desmond	D. O.	27323X	PRP	SALOPS Recce Flight			Operational Call Sign, ALPHA 3
06	Anthony	Michael	M.	8806W	PRP	Mazoe Valley Flight	VP-YWD ZS-EWD	PA-28 Cherokee 180B Cessna 210	Outpost July '64, p8 (plus the piper Cherokee that he used as Copper 9); Outpost Aug '75, p.20; Outpost Feb '78, p7 (photo).
154	Ashworth	Michael	M. G.	14188W	PRP	PGHQ Sby	VP-WCS	Cessna 210A	
	Austin		L. S.	17846X	PRO				
36	Bales-Smith	William 'Bill'	W.	2845E		Lomagundi Flight			2845R noted as J. Ward
	Ball	John	J. S.	10395Y	PRP	Manicaland Flight	VP-YVG	PA-18A Super Cub 150	Call sign CHEETAH 3
34	Barker	James (Jim)	J. M.	10328A	PRP	Lomagundi Flight	VP-YKA	Piper 32-300 Cherokee Six	Karoi Farmer, received the Police Distinguished Gallantry Award in 1970 when serving with PATU. Phillips' History of the BSAP calls it the 'Commissioner's Gallantry Award' but this is incorrect. Wrote the book Paradise Plundered. Call sign noted as BRONCO 2
	Barnett	Cecil	C.	14559Z	PRO				Awarded Commissioner's Commendation for Bravery for support of a security patrol in the Wankie area in 1967. Outpost Dec '67 (photo).
04	Barton	Walter Hutcheons	W. H.	12274Q	PRP	Mazoe Valley Flight	VP-WIV; VP-YXZ	Cessna 182P; Cessna 182H	Mount Darwin, Outpost July '79, p.23
164	Bater	Rod	R. W. I.	24632Y	PRP	Midlands Flight			BSAP F/R 1964-69, R/P/O driving B cars with Traffic Branch 1969–74, PRAW 1974–1980 (Force No. 16865F), PRAW Training Officer, last person in the unit to hold the responsibility of training / assessing PRAW pilots. Served with the Zimbabwe Police Air Wing
115	Bell	Peter	P. R.	3463N	PRO	Marandellas Flight, Mazoe Valley Flight 1970	VP-YJX	Auster 5	Farmer in Mrewa
	Bell		G. B. M.	11500Z	PRO				Mashonaland

Copper No	Surname	Name	Initials	Force No	Pilot/Obs	Flight	Registration	Aircraft	Notes (*continued*)
	Benetar	Solly	S.			PGHQ Sby.?	VP-YRS	PA-32-260 Cherokee	Flew with Roy Anderson, shared ownership of VP-YRS. Mentioned as being in Air Wing in Outpost Aug 1975, p.30
	Beniston	James	J. M.	15277E	PRO				
234	Benjamin	Howard Julian	H. J.	29194G	PRP	PGHQ Sby			General Manager of his own company, National Avionics Pvt. Ltd, during which time he developed a VHF direction finding system that was installed in some PRAW aircraft to track down insurgents, using miniature transmitters planted in radios.
	Bensusan	Arthur	A.				VP-YPZ	PA-22 Tri-pacer 160	Mining Consultant, owned Gladstone Mine, Arcturus. Ex RAF Pilot, killed on 12th February 1979 when Air Rhodesia Flight RH827, Viscount 'Umniati' YP-YND, was shot down – Ref: Umniati Roll of Honour on internet.
	Berk	Ernie	E. R.	380149E	PRP	PGHQ Sby	VP-YUJ VP-WCS	Cessna 182A Cessna 210	A Company Director, Outpost Apr 78, p.29 (photo).
71	Bickle	Colin Lancaster	C. L.	12186V	PRP	Matabeleland Flight	VP-WIL	Cessna TU.206F	Matabeleland Flight Commander until succeeded by Mike Garde. Also, Copper 111 and call sign DUIKER 2. Andrew Watson (son of Doc Watson) sent the following: 'Colin Bickle had a C-206, which he wrote off at when he tried to pull the prop through while the mags were on and the engine stated and the plane moved off by itself'
31	Boltt	Charles Richard	C. R.	5791T	PRP	Lomagundi Flight	VP-YUG	Cessna 172C	In the Northern Rhodesia Frontier Force during WWII. Area Manager of an Insurance Co in Sinoia. Awarded Commissioner's Special Commendation for Bravery. Nickname 'Dickie'. Deputy Flight Commander, Lomagundi Flight, call sign noted as BRONCO 3. Outpost Mar '69, p.12 (photo)
155	Bondi	Isaac	I	14228P	PRP	PGHQ Sby			Outpost Apr '78, p29 (photo)
158	Bradley	Brian	B. A. F.	15281J	PRP	PGHQ Sby			Dress uniform passed on to Shelagh Anderson, re-tailored to suit. Uniform now in WMK collection

Copper No	Surname	Name	Initials	Force No	Pilot/Obs	Flight	Registration	Aircraft	Notes (*continued*)
	Bradshaw	John	F. J. S.	11114E	PRP	Lomagundi Flight			Paradise Plundered by Jim Barker, p.171 (photo). Was an Observer in the 1974 roll
	Bradshaw		R. J.	15118G	PRO				Noted as a Stick Leader at some stage
	Breeze		D. T.	16941N	PRO				
40	Brink		D. J.	19096F	PRP	Lomangundi Flight			
	Brittlebank	Percy Philip	P. P.	14240C	PRP		VP-YUY	PA-22 Tri-pacer 135	Awarded Commissioner's Commendation for Bravery for support of a security patrol in the Wankie area in 1967. Outpost Dec '67 (photo). Runner up in the Commissioner's Trophy 1965 with PRO Barnett, winners were the RRAF.
163	Brown	'Buster'	R. C.	16827P	PRP	SALOPS Recce Flight	VP-WFO	Cessna TP-206B	SALOPS Operational Call sign ALPHA 0, TP.206 was armed for SALOPS armed sorties. (Ref. Grierson and Tony Mann). Also Copper 280. Also PGHQ Flight June 1978
14	Brown		S. B.	14760S	PRP	Mazoe Valley Flight			Was he PRP, medals list PRO
	Brown	Strath	J. S.	14326W	PRO	PGHQ Sby	VP-YXO	Mooney M.20E	He taught all five of his children to fly. He entered more than 30 Zimbabwe Air Rallies, sometimes as a pilot, and sometimes as a navigator for one of his children or other young and enthusiastic pilots, winning the event three times. He owned over the years a Mooney, a Piper Super Cub and Cessna 210. A member of the Salisbury Flight, and later the Lomagundi Flight.
	Brown			7376	PRP	Matabeleland Flight			Awarded Commissioners Commendation in 1962, along with PRO Magee. Possibly Ken Brown noted in Outpost Jul 1964 as winner of the Commissioner's Trophy with PRO George Magee of Salisbury. Outpost Nov '62 p.38
	Brown	Anthony	J. A.	14506R	PRP				
130	Browne	Tony ?	V. A. D.	9022F	PRP	Midlands Flight			Flight Commander.
	Browning	Mike	M. W.	17490K	PRO	Manicaland Flight			Outpost April '75, cover (photo)
	Burgess		P. M.	17277D	PRO				

Copper No	Surname	Name	Initials	Force No	Pilot/Obs	Flight	Registration	Aircraft	Notes (*continued*)
	Butler	David	D		PRP	Manicaland Flight			Cessna 172? Member of the Rhodesia Party, an Olympic Yachtsman, killed in a car accident in Belgium during Olympic trials. Could be 7267 Y D., or 18853 R. D. V. Butler
63	Carswell	Alan 'Jock'	A. C.	29206V		Marandellas Flight			Medal to F/R
	Cartwright	David	C. D.	18769A	PRO	Marandellas Flight	VP-WFM	PA-32-300 Cherokee	Joined Air wing about June 1976. Flew in the Marandellas flight, when Hugh Chisnall was Flight Commander. After training at Darwin, Cartwright and the late Nigel Challoner were accepted as recce pilots.
112	Challoner		H.	18796E	PRP	Marandellas Flight			Nigel?
88	Chandler	Ronald	B. R. H.	24517Y	PRP	Matabeleland Flight	VP-WFC	Cessna P.206A	
	Chappe de Leonval	Paul Thomas Lafitte	P.	10741Z	PRP		ZS-IYN	Cessna 206	Flew armed aircraft, one using an FN, and a Cessna 186 using a machine gun mounted in the doorway.
122	Cherry	Timothy Andrew	T. A. 'Tim'	22303R	PRO	Matabeleland			Ex Regular. Magistrate in Que Que in the mid-1970s. Aircraft known as 'Tipsy Nipper', member of Que Que Flying Club.
110	Chisnall	Hugh	H. V.	6110Q	PRP	Marandellas Flight, Mazoe Valley Flight 1970	VP-YLE	Tri-pacer in 1962	Mrewa, Flight Commander Marandellas Flight from its formation c1973
114	Church		P. F.	20931A	PRP	Marandellas Flight			
170	Cleveland	Gerry	G. M.	9151W	PRP	SALOPS Recce Flight			SALOPS Operational call sign ALPHA 1, also Copper 281. PGHQ Flight June 1978.
53	Connor	John	J. B.	20912X	PRP	Manicaland Flight	VP-YWA(2)	Cessna 210H	Manicaland PRAW Deputy Flight Commander in 1980, also Copper 52 [1978] and call sign CHEETAH 4 in 1974
02	Cowan	Henry	H.	11103S	PRP	PGHQ Sby			Deputy Unit Commander in 1978. Call sign noted as LEO 2 Outpost Oct '76, p20 (photo).
	Crowley	Kevin	K. L.	14574Q	PRP	Victoria Flight	VP-WIM	Reims/Cessna FR.172G Rocket	
62	Currin	Cyril	C. C.	27524R		Manicaland Flight	VP-WFK	Cessna 210	
176	Danes	Norman	N. D.	26950S	PRP	PGHQ Sby			

Copper No	Surname	Name	Initials	Force No	Pilot/Obs	Flight	Registration	Aircraft	Notes (*continued*)
86	Darlow		R. G. E.	21995G	PRP	Matabeleland Flight			Served 1976 until around Feb 1979, when he joined Air Rhodesia. Flew for four months as an Observer with Pat Wesson in Partenavia P64 VP-WEJ. First call up as PRAW pilot was 30 March 1977 in PA28-235 VP-YKD. Flew Partenaivia VP-WEJ, on PRAW duties
162	Davenport	Robert	R. E.	19180X	PRP	PGHQ Sby			Flew with Alan Murray (ref. Shelagh Anderson)
95	Davies	Alan	A. C.	23355K	PRP	Victoria Flight	VP-WFV	PA-32-300 Cherokee	
	Davis		A. L. N.	17150Q	PRO				
91	Davy		C. B.	13983Y		Victoria Flight			
10	Dawson	Mike John	M. J.	7231J	PRP	Mazoe Valley Flight	VP-YXW	PA-28-180C Cherokee	M. L. J.? Outpost Feb '78, p.7 (photo)
	Daykin		S. R. R.	10711R	PRO	Marandellas Flight			Was with Lomagundi Flight March 1974
08	Dax	Hamilton Fenner	H. F. 'Hammy'	4735W	PRP	Mazoe Valley Flight	VP-YYL	PA-24-260B Comanche	Farmer in Centenary area, Everton farm. Past 'Tobacco Grower of the Year'. Died pf cancer 3 January 2005 in Pietermaritzburg. Outpost Oct '75, cover (photo); Outpost July '79 p.23
	de Jongh	Louis	L. J.	13253E	PRO	Marandellas Flight			Mashonaland Observer for N B Pritchard
	Dean	Robin	R. B.	17955Q	PRP	Marandellas Flight			Reims
	Dodds-Brooks	Shaw	S. H.	14918P	PRO	Marandellas Flight	VP-WGM	Cessna 182J Skylane	
35	Donald	George	G. W.	9131Z	PRP	Lomagundi Flight	ZS-KBG	Cessna 206	Cessna 206. Mentioned in an article in Outpost Jan '76, p.6. Paradise Plundered by Jim Barker, p.171 (photo). Initially an Observer, call sign BRONCO 4.
	Donnelly	Francis Joseph	F. J.	6828W	PRP	Lomagundi Flight		Cessna 182	Known as Frank. Call sign BRONCO 5. Paradise Plundered by Jim Barker, p.171 (photo). Aircraft shared with Abby Williams-Wynne who was not a member of PRAW.
120	Downey	Paul	L. P.	23347B	PRP	Marandellas Flight			
	Ellison		D. T.	19607	PRO	Matabeleland Flight			
	Elliot	Doug	D. G.	34054P	PRP	SALOPS Recce Flight			Flew VP-YJX. Assigned specific reconnaissance duties, not involved with armed aircraft (Ref. T. Mann)

Copper No	Surname	Name	Initials	Force No	Pilot/Obs	Flight	Registration	Aircraft	Notes (*continued*)
123	Elliot-Darlow	'Poogie'	R. G.	17331M		Matabeleland Flight	VP-WAI, later became Z-WAI	Cessna 206	17331M appears to have been a F/R initially, Flew the Liebig's C.206 (ref. Andrew Watson)
98	Engles		L. T.	15709Z	PRP	Victoria Flight	VP-WFE	Cessna 337C	
	Ewart	Kevin	K.		PRP		VP-WBG	PA-32-260 Cherokee	Possibly 12542G F/R Kevin Ewart
83	Farewell-Roberts	Len	L.	21908M	PRP	Matabeleland Flight		C-206	Also Copper 79? 119; Len or Leonard? Surname also noted as just Roberts
75	Fenner	Roger	R.	22564A	PRP	Matabeleland Flight			Copper 113?
89	Ferguson	Ian	W. A. I.	16172C		Matabeleland Flight	VP-WGK	PA-32-260 Cherokee	Copper 125? Was F/R when awarded RGSM
191	Fernandes	Bob	G. R. L.	23688X	PRP	Matabeleland Flight			Copper 127?
	Filmer		H.			Mazoe Valley Flight			Shown in 1970 photograph of the Mazoe Valley Flight – Possibly F/R 4565 L HW Filmer
	Ford		A.		PRP	Mazoe Valley Flight			
	Foreman		G. K.	7625M	PRO				
134	Fuller	Michael	M.	25578B	PRP	Midlands Flight			
70	Garde	Michael Henry	M. H.	17061T	PRP	Matabeleland Flight	VP-WIN	PA-30-160 Twin Comanche	Flight Commander, Copper 110 and call sign DUIKER 3. Killed in an air crash on 27 January 1985 in the Induna Training Area, Bulawayo, he was in a Beech Musketeer Z-WAE with Mark Einhorn (the owner) and Mark's girlfriend. Garde was believed to have been practising for an instructor rating
167	Gardner	Mike	M.		PRP?	Matabeleland Flight, then PGHQ Flight?			Joined PRAW in 1974 based in Bulawayo and then in Salisbury
	Gibson		G. D.	18733L	PRO				
	Gibson	David	D. E.	7936A	PRO	Manicaland Flight			Geoff Gibson in Outpost Feb '78, p.7 (photo)
	Gowan		H.		PRP				Noted as a Flight Commander in Outpost Dec 1970
	Graham	Allan Albert	A. A.	14612G	PRP				
	Graham-Owen	Lester James	L. J.	10283B	PRP				
80	Grant	Kenneth	K. J.	21223S	PRP	Manicaland Flight			Also Copper 56 [1978]
	Graves		P. W.	3009S		Victoria Flight			

Copper No	Surname	Name	Initials	Force No	Pilot/Obs	Flight	Registration	Aircraft	Notes (*continued*)
73	Griffin	Milton Lionel	M. L.	9391G	PRP	Matabeleland Flight			Call sign DUIKER 4
111	Grobler	Paul	P. S.	10587G	PRP	Marandellas Flight			Paul and his wife Mary were ambushed by insurgents while trying to take off in their Cessna 310P. They both survived the atack
	Grobler	Steven	S. P.	19780Z	PRP	Marandellas Flight			
55	Gunn	Peter	P.	14819G	PRP	Manicaland Flight			
	Haasbroek	Ferdie	F.	16201J		Lomagundi Flight			Copper 40?, Mhangura – F/R on RGSM.
13	Haasbroek	Charl Francois 'Sarel'	C. F.	11473V	PRP	Mazoe Valley Flight	VP-YYF	PA-28-180CCherokee	Umvukwes, Doma.
32	Hacking	Bertram Cecil William	B. C. W.	9687D	PRP	Lomagundi Flight	VP-YWH	Cessna 172E	Call sign BRONCO 6. Karoi. 'Paradise Plundered' by Jim Barker, p157, p.171 (photo).
171	Hall		P. N.	23862L	PRP	PGHQ Sby			
	Hamilton		J. R.	10139V	PRO				Mashonaland
167	Hammond	Ed 'Wally'	E. G.	24974V	PRP	PGHQ Sby			
	Harris	James	J.	9172					Outpost Nov '65 p.16
92	Harrison	Eric	E. R.	18290T		Victoria Flight	VP-YJA(2)	Cessna 182	
74	Hart	John	P. D.	15226Z	PRP	Matabeleland Flight			Call sign DUIKER 5. Previously an Observer, Ref Outpost Feb '73. John died in 2016
132	Harty		D. P.	17780A	PRP	Midlands Flight			
113	Harvey	George James William	G. J. W.	20932B	PRP	Marandellas Flight SALOPS Flight			Ex RAF, Deputy Unit Commander and Flight Commander SALOPS Flight – Ex Regular Supt. 4617
178	Heap	John	J. R.	25099F		PGHQ Sby			Flying Standards Flight
84	Henderson		I. M.	8523N	PRP	Matabeleland Flight		C-206	Copper 120?
58	Hilderbrand	Rupert	R. C.	16836Z	PRP	Manicaland Flight	VP-WAV	Cessna 185	
	Hole		E. D.	17398T	PRP				
150	Holland	Don	D. V.	14401C	PRP	PGHQ Sby			Flight Commander of PGHQ Flight before Roy Anderson
129	Hollins	Ray	R.	22953Y		Matabeleland Flight	VP-WHL; VP-WDC	Reims/Cessna FR.172J Rocket; PA-22 Colt 108	F/R on RGSM
76	Honman	John Oliver	J. O.	5336T	PRP	Matabeleland Flight			
54	Howard	Donald (Don)	D. W.	19804A	PRP	Manicaland Flight	VP-WIT	PA-28R-200 Cherokee Arrow	Call sign CHEETAH 5. Outpost April '75, cover (photo)

Copper No	Surname	Name	Initials	Force No	Pilot/Obs	Flight	Registration	Aircraft	Notes (*continued*)
50	Howell	David	D. L. M.	6558C	PRP	Manicaland Flight			Flight Commander 1970. Call Sign CHEETAH 1. Outpost Dec '70 & 1978 – PRLSM 30 March 1973. Died 26 December 2002
16	Hurley	Victor	V.	14495E	PRP	Mazoe Valley Flight			Centenary
133	James	Peter	P. L.	21517M	PRP	Midlands Flight			
	Jameson	Derek Bruce	D. B.	5014Z	PRO				
	Jellicoe	Leslie Malcolm	L. M. 'Les'	14681G	PRP	Mazoe Valley Flight			Centenary M.S.M. received posthumously by his widow Mrs Elizabeth May Jellicoe and his son Stewart Frank Jellicoe. Outpost July '79 p.23.
	Johnson	Dave	D. A.	20635D		PGHQ Sby			
18	Johnson	Pat	P. C.	17493N		Mazoe Valley Flight			
	Jones		G. M.	17395G	PRO				
	Jordan		R. A.	15035R	PRP				
	Keith		B. M.	20568F	PRO				
	Kennedy	Joseph	J. L.	30587W		Midlands Flight			
	King	Des	D.	18339	PRO	SALOPS Recce Flight			
50	Kluckow	Ian	I. A.	19207B		Lomagundi Flight	VP-WIZ	Cessna 182L	Doma – F/R on RGSM
72	Knight	Oliver	O. H. 'Ollie'	13747R	PRP	Matabeleland Flight	VP-WEG; VP-YYT	Cessna U.206C; Cessna 172	Outpost Feb '83, also Copper 25, BSAP Roll 1974, Call sign DUIKER 7
77	Knight	Aiden	M. A.	17765J	PRP	Matabeleland Flight	VP-WEG	Cessna U.206C	Bulawayo – BSAP Roll Calls Sign DUIKER 6
	Lawton	Alfred 'Dendy'	A. D.	13970J	PRP		VP-YUI	Beech A35 Bonanza	Killed on active service in an air accident 6 May 1967, Beechcraft Bonanza, Umtali.
	Liebenberg		C. F.	5721	PRP	Matabeleland Flight			Call sign DUIKER 8
121	Linfield	William 'Bill'	G. W. R.	25829Z	PRP	Marandellas Flight	VP-WGM	Cessna 182J Skylane	Ex Regular, Chief Inspector 5652, Flight Commander, Unit Commander 1982-2004
	Lloyd-Roberts	Glynn	G.	29647		PGHQ Sby			
03	Ludgater	William John 'Bill'	W. J.	6282C	PRP	Mazoe Valley Flight	VP-YTV and VP-YWL(2)	Cessna 180F	Flight Commander, died in an aircraft crash, together with his wife and Phillipa Berlyn en route to Kariba. Outpost Feb '78, p.7 (photo)

Copper No	Surname	Name	Initials	Force No	Pilot/Obs	Flight	Registration	Aircraft	Notes (*continued*)
	Lyon	Dougie	D. H.	6477P	PRO	Mazoe Valley Flight			Born in Scotland, 17 December 1922. After farming near Kirriemuir in Perthshire joined the RAF during WWII, trained in Canada, served in India and Burma. Emigrated to Rhodesia as a farm assistant, and subsequently bought the farm, Leopards Vlei, in the Glendale
12	MacDonald	William Alastair Ross	W. A. R.	5145R	PRP		VP-YUG	Cessna 172C	Ex RAF, DFC for 7 confirmed kills and numerous ground attack successes. Left RAF as Squadron Leader. Tobacco farmer in Arcturus and Sinoia Districts. Awarded the Commissioner's Special Commendation for Bravery after rescuing a lost SAP Policeman.
152	Magee	John Herbert	J. H.	6998F	PRP	PGHQ Sby., Matabeleland Flight 1962			Noted as PRO in Outpost Nov '58. Awarded Commissioner's Commendation in 1962 along with 7379 PRP Brown. Outpost Nov '62
19	Main		T. F.	8504S		Mazoe Valley Flight	VP-YJF	Auster J/5F Aiglet Trainer	Bindura – F/R on RGSM
282	Mann	Anthony	A. T.	31739Y	PRP	Marandellas Flight			Also SALOPS Recce Flight, Operational Call Sign ALPHA 2
	Manning	Francis Lane	F. L.	10112Q	PRP	Lomagundi Flight		Auster	Noted in Paradise Plundered by Jim Barker.
30	Manning	John Lane	J. L.	6380J	PRP	Lomagundi Flight		Cessna 172	Flight Commander Lomagundi Flight, Doma. Call sign noted as BRONCO 1. Outpost July '79, p.23; Paradise Plundered by Jim Barker pp.157 & 171 (photo).
43	Marchussen	Peter Oscar	P. O.	22124X	PRP	Lomagundi Flight			Doma
	Martin		A. C.	24747Y	PRO				
	Marzorati	John Edward	J. E.		PRP				Squadron Leader Southern Rhodesian Air Forces and RAFVR MBE, London Gazette 1 January 1944. Outpost Dec '57 with Roy Smart's VP-YGZ, Copper 1 Mr J. E. Marzorati, of Bulawayo, was appointed as Assistant Director of Works and Supplies for the building of Kumalo Airport with the rank of Flight Lieutenant
166	Maurice		K. G.	21803Y	PRP	PGHQ Sby			
49	McGrath	Michael Barry	M. B.	10359J		Lomagundi Flight			Was F/R.

Copper No	Surname	Name	Initials	Force No	Pilot/Obs	Flight	Registration	Aircraft	Notes (*continued*)
178	McKenzie	Bruce	B.						Outpost Nov '74, p.21 noted as ex PRAW
12	Middleton		H. I.	21608L		Mazoe Valley Flight			Bindura
177	Miller		P.	27559E	PRP	PGHQ Sby			
39	Moorcroft	Sidney	S. A.	18740T		Lomagundi Flight	ZS-DIT	Cessna 206	
33	More	Eric	E.	15469	PRP	Chipinga Flight			
	Morton		H. J. W.	13805E	RPO				
45	Mullock-Bentley	Desmond Ponsonby	D. P.	12185T		Lomagundi Flight	ZS-IWN	Cessna 182	
161	Murray	Alan	A.	17819S	PRP	PGHQ Sby	VP-WEE; VP-YOT(2)	Cessna 177 Cardinal; Cessna 210D, possibly armed	A jeweller. Also Copper 282 & 243. SALOPS Recce Flight PR 45/L/2. Outpost April '78, p.4 (photo) with VP-WEE.
	Murray-Smith		W.		PRP		VP-YRB	Luscombe 8E Silvaire	Copper 2. Outpost Dec '57.
	Murrel	Ken	K.		PRP				Awarded DFM in WWII , Chief Pilot RUAC in 1975 when he won the 'Pat Judson Trophy'. Outpost July '62 p.8 (photo)
	Munch		A. M.	25906H		Manicaland Flight	VP-WCU	Cessna 172	
79	Needham	Robert	R. J. A.	17292X	PRP	Matabeleland Flight	ZS-GBL		Flying Standards Flight, Copper 115?
93	Nell	Barry	B. J.	20322N		Victoria Flight	VP-WHW	Cessna 185A Skywagon	
	Nueman		W. K.	20598	PRO	Matabeleland Flight			
	Nightingale		H. W.	16714R	PRO				
160	Nobes	Philip	P. A.	17900F	PRP	PGHQ Sby			Flight Instructor with TechAir (later with RUAC, then Affretair, flying freighters). Acceptance flight with Paul Rawson 16 January 1974 in Cherokee 140 VP-YYY. Flew numerous aircraft including Cherokee 180, Piper Aztec VP-WDE, Cessna 182, Cessna 206, Cessna 21
	Noel		R. A.	383476		Midlands Flight			
80	Norval	Warwick Phillip	W. P.	11399D	PRP	Matabeleland Flight	VP-WEY	Reims/Cessna FR.172J Rocket	Copper 116?
33	Oates	Anthony	D. A.	13246X	PRP	Lomagundi Flight	VP-WEH	Mooney M.20F	Murdered, Trelawny June 2000 – RGSM as F/R
100	Olds	Gordon	G. R.	4811D	PRO	Victoria Flight			Victoria Province
	Owen		G.			Mazoe Valley Flight			Shown in 1970 photograph of the Mazoe Valley Flight
	Page	Mike	M. V.	6879B	PRO				

Copper No	Surname	Name	Initials	Force No	Pilot/Obs	Flight	Registration	Aircraft	Notes (*continued*)
01	Palmer	Phillip	P. P.	7006P	PRP	PGHQ Sby			Deputy Director of Civil Aviation, Unit Commander 1957-1980. Call sign noted as LEO 1 Outpost Oct 76, p.20 (photo); Jan 78, p32.
292	Parish		G. P. J.	24065G	PRP	SALOPS Recce Flight			Assigned specific reconnaissance duties, not involved with armed Aircraft (Ref. T. Mann)
	Parker		L. G.	7626N	PRO	Matabeleland Flight			
131	Parker	Ernest	E.	8324X	PRP	Midlands Flight			Hartley
59	Pascall		R. C.	17176T	PRO	Manicaland Flight			PRO as per 1974 roll
05	Pascoe	Ronald Geoffrey 'Ronnie'	R. G.	6196J	PRP	Mazoe Valley Flight	VP-WIA; VP-YVL	Cessna U.206F; Cessna 172D	Bindura, Outpost Feb '78, p.7 (photo) . Died c2015. Wife was a W/F/R,
174	Patterson	Roger	R. J.	21407S	PRP	PGHQ Sby			Outpost Jan '78, p.4 (photo)
	Paxton		D. H.	22014C	PRO				
	Pearce		G. D.		PRO				Unit Aviation Engineer
	Perkins	William 'Bill'	W. T.	8033F	PRO	Manicaland Flight			Manicaland. Sustained burns in the crash which killed Alfred Denty Lawton
38	Philips		N. R.	9212M		Lomagundi Flight			
156	Plant	John	J. F.	15333Q	PRP	Standards Flight			Ex Fleet Air Arm, joined PRAW in early 1966 with Sby Flight, was later Flight Commander with the Standards Flight and Unit Commander 1980–1982. Copper 01.
78	Plaskett		W. E.	17505B	PRP	Matabeleland Flight			
36	Postlethwayt		C. W. G.	15923G	PRP	Lomangundi Flight			Paradise Plundered' by Jim Barker, p.171. Shared an aircraft with George Donald BRONCO 4.
	Potgieter		J. L.	16541D	PRP	Lomangundi Flight			
	Price		Dick						Outpost Jul '62 p.8
284	Pringle	Ian	I. N.	20159L	PRP	SALOPS Recce Flight			Operational call sign ALPHA 4
	Prior		T. R.	11258L	PRO				Matabeleland
	Pritchard	Neville	N. B.	13053M	PRO	Marandellas Flight			Flew VP-WIF armed with the gun mounted laterally behind the front seats, firing from the port side. Ref. Arnold Woolley.
	Purkis		C. S.	20308Y	PRO				
	Puzey	Clive	C.				ZS-EWH	Cessna C182	A City Councillor

Copper No	Surname	Name	Initials	Force No	Pilot/Obs	Flight	Registration	Aircraft	Notes *(continued)*
	Quinn		J.	22015D	PRO				
157	Rawson	Paul	P. C.	9689F	PRP	PGHQ Sby., Mazoe Valley Flight 1970			Flying Standards Flight Commander; Outpost Mar '80 p.29 (photo [poor])
	Rayner	Peter	P.			Marandellas Flight	ZS-EZZ	Cessna C182	
	Reed	Bruce	B.		PRO	Mazoe Valley Flight			Outpost Feb '78, p7 (photo)
	Reid		B. B.	7846C	PRO				
	Reville	John	J.	17954P	PRO	Mazoe Valley Flight			Born in Derbyshire in 1938, moved to Kenya with his parents in 1952. Joined the Kenyan Police Force after leaving school. Moved to Rhodesia in 1969 where he opened a garage, joined Pol Res in 1971, joining PATU. Later became a PRAW Observer. Killed in action, 28 June 1979
	Rex	Paul	P.	7056	PRP				PRP in March 1958, one of 19, ex RAF. Flight Commander in 1962
41	Richards	Peter	P. W.	22006T	PRP	Lomagundi Flight	VP-WDM	Cessna 172D	Noted in Paradise Plundered by Jim Barker. Farmed in Karoi before a spell in Angola, later returned to Rhodesia where he bought Ashton Farm near the Angwa River.
290	Roberts		A. J. H.	30118L	PRP	SALOPS Recce Flight			Assigned specific reconnaissance duties, not involved with armed Aircraft (Ref. T. Mann)
172	Rogers	'Pip'	J.P.	22490V	PRP	PGHQ Sby			Outpost Jul '62 p.8
	Rogers	David	D.	4062P	PRP				
117	Sainsbury	Robert	R. W. J.	21053H	PRP	Marandellas Flight			
	Saunders	Sandy	E.	2714B	PRP	PGHQ Sby			
50	Scales	Peter Frank	P. F.	8909H	PRP	Matabeleland Flight	VP-WCV	Stinson 108-1 Voyager	Noted as a Flight Commander in Outpost Dec '70, and in 1974 roll with call sign DUIKER 1
	Seward	Richard	B. R. T.	6215E	PRO				Deputy Unit Commander 1982-2000 – Chipinga
179	Sherwood	Ray?	R. V.	25100G		PGHQ Sby			Flying Standards Flight
	Short	Robert	R.						
17	Simon	Eden	E.	14520G	PRP	Mazoe Valley Flight	VP-WHR	Cessna 182F	Bindura, also flown by R Hollins

Copper No	Surname	Name	Initials	Force No	Pilot/Obs	Flight	Registration	Aircraft	Notes (*continued*)
81	Simpson	Mike	M. H.	19611Q	PRP	Matabeleland Flight			Originally Copper 81. Joined in 1972 as Observer for Ollie Knight, Pilot in Sept 1974, Matabeleland Prov Standards Officer 1980–84 when he retired. Copper 117
286	Simpson	Peter	P.	31819K	PRP	SALOPS Recce Flight			Operational Call Sign ALPHA 6
	Simpson		R. L.	19382R	PRO	Matabeleland Flight			
	Smart	Roy	G. R.	4031	PRP	Manicaland Flight 1958	VP-YGZ; VP-YRD	Beech 35 Bonanza; Beech Bonanza Model K	Rusape. Ex Regular 3101, twice winner of the State Lottery. Attested Squad 2/29, discharged in 1935. Awarded an MBE in the New Year Honours List in 1963. Outpost July '62 p.8 (photo); Outpost Feb '63 p.39 (photo);
07	Smith	Rob	R. P.	3520A	PRP	Mazoe Valley Flight			Possibly Ray Smith, Copper 9, of Bindura pictured in Outpost July '64 p.8
60	Smith	Johannes	J. J.	16632G		Manicaland Flight	VP-WFA	Cessna T-207	
85	Smith		A. N.	21611P	PRP	Matabeleland Flight			Copper 121?
	Smith		H. S. C.	23968B	PRO				
	Soul	John			PRO				Flew as Chris Thorne's observer/gunner
	Springer	William 'Bill'	W. J.	3480	PRP	Manicaland Flight	VP-YNR	Auster J/5	Flight Commander Manicaland Flight, ran a garage in Chipinga. Killed on Active Service in an Air Accident 19 July 1969, Cessna 172. Outpost Jul '64 p.8 (photo)
	Stam	George Angelos	A. G.	11104T	PRP	PGHQ?			Attested 10 April 1961. Killed on active service in an air accident, 23 February 1978. RoH Outpost Mar '78.
	Stanning	Thomas Ripley	T. R.	5685D	PRO				Mashonaland
118	Steed	John	J. F.	20787T	PRP	Marandellas Flight	VP-WFY	Cessna 182M Skylane	Author of Cowboys don't Fly
91	Steel	John (known as Ian)	J. A.	29201P	P/R/P	Manicaland Flight	VP-WFK	Cessna 210	
	Stevenson		C. G.	13158B	PRO				Midlands
	Stockley		D. J.	22145V	PRO				
	Strever	Edward Theodore	E. T.	16034C	PRP				
90	Style	Rodney Elliot	R. E.	8899X	PRP	Victoria Flight	VP-WCL	Cessna 182L	Flight Commander June 1978. Outpost July '79 p.23
	Style	Louis	L.	9517		PGHQ Sby			

Copper No	Surname	Name	Initials	Force No	Pilot/Obs	Flight	Registration	Aircraft	Notes (*continued*)
97	Style	Clive	C. S.	8653E	PRP	Victoria Flight	VP-WHD	Cessna U.206E	
101	Szechenyi		C.	26870F		Victoria Flight			
96	Tayler	John	R. J.	23356L	PRP	Victoria Flight			Farmer at M'Kwasine. Flew Alistair Davies's Cherokee 6 Cherokee 6 PA 32-300, VP-WFV
	Taylor		T. A.	20097T	PRO				
	Thompson		A. S. C.	21882J	PRO	Matabeleland Flight			
	Thompson		T. D.	25909L		Manicaland Flight	VP-WFN	Cessna 182F	
15	Thorne	Chris	C. J.	24996T	PRP	Mazoe Valley Flight	N9013M	Cessna 180H	Bindura, armed with a Browning
180	Thorne	Peter	P. B.	24827K	PRP	PGHQ Sby			
	van Aardt		F.	18145X	PRO	Manicaland Flight			
57	van Buuren	Brian Anthony	B. A.	9047H	PRP	Manicaland Flight	ZS-JUM	Cessna 210K Turbo	Flight Commander – Outpost July '79 p.23
	Van der Merwe		M. M.	17270W	PRO	Lomagundi Flight			
190	Van der Reit	Rupert	R. T.	19684V	PRP	Matabeleland Flight			Copper 126?
	van Jaarsveldt		A. B.	14943R	PRO				
	van Niekerk	Andy	A.	23940W	PRO				Flew with Peter Anderson, very good knowledge of Kariba
	Venter		D. T.	20845G	PRO				
	Vermaak	Martin	J. M.	2624B	PRO				Victoria Province
173	Visagie	Gerald	G. J.	27579B	PRP	PGHQ Sby			
61	Von Landsberg		J. P.	25910M		Manicaland Flight			
	Walker		M. A.	23166E	PRO				
11	Waller	Noel Thornburg	N. T.	12296P	PRP	Mazoe Valley Flight			Known as 'Bundu', he was a spotter for Wally Barton, after attaining 475 hours he was accepted as a PRAW pilot. From Centenary. Outpost July '79 p.23
44	Walton	Peter	P. P.	19214J	PRO	Lomagundi Flight			Farmed outside Sinoia, near Sinoia caves, PRO; an artist who did some BSAP uniform paintings. Flew with a farmer from Mangula. Possibly a PRP in 1978
94	Warne		W.	15018Y	PRP	Victoria Flight			
192	Watson		J. R.	27065S	PRP	Matabeleland Flight	VP-WHM	Beech V35 Bonanza	Also Copper 128?, lived in the Gwanda area. Beech Bonanza VP-WHM with gun pods under the wings, fitted by Matabele Air in Bulawayo in 1979

Copper No	Surname	Name	Initials	Force No	Pilot/Obs	Flight	Registration	Aircraft	Notes (*continued*)
82	Wesson	Patrick	P. J. H.	7107Z	PRP	Matabeleland Flight			Transferred from PATU into PRAW Jan 1975, first flying W. R. Croukamp's Partenavia P64 VP-WEJ, and then ZS-KEV Cherokee 6. Resigned from PRAW October 1984 and relocated to Botswana.
99	Whenham	Peter	P. S.	20174C	PRP	Victoria Flight			Cessna 337
	Whitehead	Don	D.		PRO				Outpost Feb '79 p.5 (photo)
	Whyte	Douglas	D.						
14	Wiggins						VP-YNR	Auster J/5	Outpost July '62 p.8 (photo)
37	Wilcox	Clifford	C. H.	8501P	PRP	Lomagundi Flight	ZS-IOF	Cessna 182	Karoi. Mentioned in an article on Outpost Jan '76, p.6. Citation for his action during Kariba convoy attack
	Willemse		J.	27618T	PRP	Manicaland Flight			
	Willers		H. M.	16727L		Manicaland Flight			
164	Wilson	Peter	P. H. G.	22161M	PRP	SALOPS Recce Flight	ZS-IFD	Cessna 310P	Also Copper 228 & 288 [SALOPS Flight], PGHQ Flight PR45/L/2, flew Cane Air Cessna 310. Outpost Jan '79, p3 (photo)
	Wilson	John	J.		PRP	Matabeleland Flight			Tjolotjo – flew C-172, VP-YYT
	Winter	Alan	A. R.	16518D	PRO	Matabeleland Flight			Observed for Bob Needham and was the artist who painted ZS-GBL on take off form a hot casevac
	Wixley		W.R.	19612	PRO	Matabeleland Flight			
	Wynne		I. L.	11581M	PRP				Served Sby Province
159	York	Geoff	G. H.	11552F	PRP	PGHQ Sby			Noted as a Flight Commander in Outpost Dec '70 p.5

Appendix II
Aircraft

Complied by Wayne Kennerley, Dave Newnham and Guy Ellis

Reg	Aircraft Type	C/N	Reg Date	Notes: Previous Registrations, Owner, Location
N9013M	Cessna 180H Skywagon	52113	1978	Built in 1970, purchased 1978 by C. J. Thorne Mazoe Wing, to Z-WMR (1980) to Zambia as Z-WMR Lusaka International to SA 2021
VP-WAG	PA-28 Cherokee 180C	2697	August 1965	N11C, L. M. Stay & D. Midegley, October 1975 to Techair (Pvt) Ltd to P. J. Worsley-Warswick – Marandellas

Reg	Aircraft Type	C/N	Reg Date	**Notes: Previous Registrations, Owner, Location** (*continued*)
VP-WAI	Cessna 172E	51755	February 1966	ZS-DWA E. A. Moore October 1975 MB Taylor Gwanda then owned by Poogie Darlow & Ronnie Pascoe, seen at Victoria Falls in 2005 as Z-WAI
VP-WAP	PA-22 Tri-Pacer 160	3950	1966	previously in Zambia as 9J-ROS (also VP-YOS), regd VP-WAP to P. Rogers, Mount Hampden. on BASP Nominal Roll of Aircraft 1 March 1974
VP-WAV	Cessna 185	0180	December 1966	ZS-CSS, N9980X, R.C. Hildebrand – Umtali
VP-WAY	Cessna 180	30841	1967	5Y-KMJ, VP-KMJ, M2941C. Later ZS-LOU (1984). J. Deere Charles Prince to C. B. Davy, Fort Victoria. Also owned by Peter Scales, Bulawayo
VP-WBC(2)	Cessna 182C	52828	June 1967	Ex N8928T, ZS-COC (1960), later Z-WBC. Mashonaland Flying Club (PRAW Rod Bater) - Charles Prince
VP-WBD	Cessna 175A Skylark	56664	August 1967	Ex N7964T, ZS-CNX (1960), R. C. Brown & J. E. Rogers to Mashonaland Flying Club (PRAW Rod Bater), Charles Prince later Z-WBD
VP-WBG	PA-32 Cherokee 260	32-773	September 1967	ZS-ESN, Kevin Ewart and D. B. Perkins . Kevin Ewart – post 1980, ADF pilot, aircraft also flown by Bill Linfield – Chipinga
VP-WCH	Cessna 180A	50082	May 1968	Previously with C. J. H. Armstrong, Pietermaritzburg, SA as ZS-CHA regd VP-WCH owner unknown, post October 1975 , sold in SA as ZS-CHA. On BASP Nominal Roll of Aircraft 1 March 1974
VP-WCI	Cessna 172	46857	May 68	Previously in the United States as N7257T, reg VP-WCI to K. M. Edwards, Karoi. On BASP Nominal Roll of Aircraft, 1 March 1974
VP-WCK	Cessna P.206C Super Skylane	0484	September 1968	Previously in SA as ZS-FFT, reg VP-WCK to H. R. Suttner, Massa. On BASP Nominal Roll of Aircraft, 1 March 1974
VP-WCL	Cessna 182L Skylane	58902	September 1968	ZS-FIAT, N42210, Rodney. E. Style – Buffalo Range
VP-WACO	PA-28R-108 Cherokee Arrow	30107	1968	Previously in Zambia as 9J-RHD, reg VP-WACO to C. J. Maltby. On BASP Nominal Roll of Aircraft, 1 March 1974
VP-WCP	Cessna 182A Skylane	34451	October 1968	Colin Bickle, ZS-CGB (1957), N3751D – regd VP-WCP in 1968 to the Mashonaland Skydivers Club. Used by SALOPS Wing in the late 1970s fitted with a Browning .303 (T. Mann). Later Z-WCP
VP-WCS	Cessna 210A	57727	1968	9J-RBK, VP-YTD, ZS-CRJ [1/61-6/61], N9427X. Mike G. Ashworth Later to P. F. Scales. Used by Ernie Berk post 1980 Z-WCS – Charles Prince
VP-WCU	Cessna 172	46345	1968	Previously in USA Identity unknown, regd VP-WCU to A.M. Munch, Umtali, 1973 with Zero 6 Flying club, Charles Prince
VP-WCV	Stinson 108-3 Voyager	4078	1965	9J-RUA, VP-RUA, VP-YUA, ZS-DEV, N6078M. P. F. Scales, ZS-JKV in 1975 – Bulawayo. Built 1947
VP-WDB	Cessna 172K	57892	September 1969	N79117 to Matabeleland Flying School, Induna. Bob Fernandes flew this on PRAW duties
VP-WDC	PA-22-108 Colt	8658	1969	9J-RRU, VP-RRU, VP-YRU. Roy Hollins (under rebuild 1982) Gwanda
VP-WDD	Cessna 172	36783	1969	W. E. Plasket Wankie Eastern Gateway Air Services To P. G. D. Hill, , Umtali
VP-WDE	PA-23-250 Aztec	27-528	September 1969	Imported into SA as ZS-CXI then to Rhodesia to Techair, Mount Hampden as VP-WDE, changed to Z-WDE then Z-BRA where it was flown in a London to Sydney Air Race by Julian Scales. Remained in Australia as VH-XBU. Used on PRAW duties by several PRAW pilots, notably Mike Gardner
VP-WDJ	Cessna 182K Skylane	57769	1970	9J-RDT, ZS-ERX. N2569Q, A.M. Alford Tony flew for PRAW – Bindura
VP-WDM	Cessna 172D	51751	1970	ZS-DWD, 9J-RDF, ZS-DWD, N7751U. P. W Richards – Karoi

Reg	Aircraft Type	C/N	Reg Date	Notes: Previous Registrations, Owner, Location (*continued*)
VP-WDR	Beech A23-24 Musketeer Super	MA-160	January 1970	Previously in SA as ZS-EYY, reg VP-WDR Techair, Bulawayo, post October 1975 reg cancelled. On BASP Nominal Roll of Aircraft, 1 March 1974
VP-WDS	PA-28-235B Cherokee	10840	1970	Previously in Ivory Coast as TU-THE, reg VP-WDS to Vic-Air Ltd, Mount Hampden, July 1973 to Vic-Air Ltd, Charles Prince, post October 1975 to P. Brummer, Chiredzi. On BASP Nominal Roll of Aircraft, 1 March 1974
VP-WEE	Cessna 177 Cardinal	00312	1973	9J-RGE, N2912X. M.M. Van der Merwe (1973) to A. Murray – Karoi; PGHQ The Outpost April 1978, p.4. M. M Van der Merwe
VP-WEG	Cessna U.206C Super Skywagon	1042	June 1974	9J-RHF, N29058. M. A. & O. H. Knight – Bulawayo
VP-WEH	Mooney M.20F	680138	1974	9J-RGX, N6855N. D. A. Oates – Trelawney Anthony Oates PRAW
VP-WEJ	Partenavia P64	32	1973	ZS-FGJ to VP-WEJ 8/73 W. R. Croukamp
VP-WEL(2)	PA-32-300 Cherokee Six	7340102	1973	regd VP-WEL to T. I. F. Sandeman, Darwendale to Roy Anderson
VP-WEY	Reims-Cessna FR.172J Rocket	0459	1974	F-BRGU. V.P. Norvall – Warwick Norvall PRAW – Induna Bulawayo
VP-WFA	Cessna T.207 Turbo Skywagon	00098	July 1974	ZS-IYG, ZS-AVB(2), N91162. J. J. Smith – Umtali ex Des Van Jaarsveld, seen at Victoria Falls 2005 as Z-WFA
VP-WFC	Cessna 206P Super Skylane	0236	July 1973	ZS-EJJ, N4636F, to R. Webb, R. C. Brown & J. E. Rogers. Then July 1975 to B. R. H. Chandler (PRAW) - Induna Bulawayo
VP-WFE	Cessna 337C Super Skymaster	0967	April 1980	7Q-YDR, N2667S. L. T. Engels (PRAW)- Chiredzi
VP-WFG	PA-23-250B Aztec	2148	Jul 73	9J-RIR to Techair, Charles Prince PRAW pilot Mike Gardner
VP-WFK	Cessna 210	57455	1975	5Y-KPE, VP-KPE, N9655T. C. C. Currin – Umtali
VP-WFM	PA-32-300 Cherokee Six	40179	May 1975	TR-LRO – R. J. Framont, Libreville, to C. D. Cartwright, Marandellas. (PRAW David Cartwright)
VP-WFN	Cessna 182F Skylane	54933	June 1975	ZS-IFE, ZS-DOX, N3533U. T. D. Thompson (PRAW) - Umtali
VP-WFO	Cessna TP.206B Turbo System	-0370	Feb 69	ZS-ETV, N4470 F. R. C. Brown and J. E. Rogers – Owned by 'Buster' Brown (PRAW) and (PRAW) Rod Bater – Charles Prince
VP-WFR	PA-28-180B Cherokee	1183	1975	Previously with I. Scott, Botswana as A2-ZHL. c.1975 regd VP-WFR to D. Midgley – Bob Needham (PRAW)
VP-WFV	PA-32-300 Cherokee Six	32-40323	1 January 1976	A2-ZHF, 9J-RHT, 5Y-AGJ. A. C. Davies (PRAW) - Chiredzi
VP-WFX	PA-28 Cherokee 180C	28-3354	April 1975	ZS-EOT (1966) canx 75 exp as VP-WFX, later Z-WFX. R. Howard – Charles Prince
VP-WFY	Cessna 182M Skylane	59422	November 1974	ZS-FPH to J. L. O'Donovan then to John Steed (PRAW)
VP-WGK	PA-32-260 Cherokee Six	31-163	1973	C9-AJK, CR-AJK, ZS-EKC, N3328W. W. A. I. Ferguson (PRAW), Beit Bridge
VP-WGM	Cessna 182J Skylane	56861	April 1975	TR-LOR, TJ-ADE, N2761F. Bill Linfield pilot Shaw Dodds-Brooks obs./pilot based at Mount Hampden / Charles Prince. Rod Bater flew this after 1980
VP-WGN	Cessna182G Skylane	55073	October 1974	ex N3673U, ZS-DRL (1963), DBR in gale at Virginia, Durban remains to Rhodesia. Later Z-WGN. Mashonaland Flying Club – Charles Prince
VP-WGU	Cessna 180F	51204	September 1976	Previously with Babillot, Gabon as TR-LKC, regd VP-WGU to R. H. W. Flynn, Fothergill Island, to GU Partnership Chipinga
VP-WGZ	PA-28R-200 Cherokee Arrow	35061	1975	7Q-YCD Bulawayo Flying Club, seen at Victoria Falls in 2005 as Z-WGZ
VP-WHB	PA-28 Cherokee 140	20273	1977	ZS-DYY, N11C. L. Lake. Owned by Risco Flying Club when (PRAW) Rod Bater – Charles Prince
VP-WHD	Cessna U.206E Stationair	01673	January 1977	ZS-KNP, ZS-ILF, N9473G. C. S. Style (Clive Style PRAW), Buffalo Range

Reg	Aircraft Type	C/N	Reg Date	Notes: Previous Registrations, Owner, Location (*continued*)
VP-WHL	Reims/Cessna FR.172J Rocket	0428	1977	TR-LSE, (D-EGJS). R. Hollins (1977) - Gwanda
VP-WHM	Beech V-35 Bonanza	D-8547	1976	9J-REJ, 7Q-YCE. Owned 1975 – 90s by J. Robin 'Doc' Watson of West Nicholson. Fitted with under wing gun pods. Returned to civilian state c1983 Z-WHM then in 1997 became ZS-SMF – West Nicholson. Sold to a US buyer and DBR on arrival
VP-WHR	Cessna 182F Skylane	54632	1968	TR-LNX, TN-AAX, TR-LLS, F-OBZT, N11B, N3232 U. E. Simon and Roy Hollins – Bindura
VP-WHS	Piper Cherokee 32-300C	40852		Previously with S. Martin, Port-Gentil, Gabon as TR-LOZ, post December 1969 regd VP-WHS to G. Brown PRAW R. D. Chandler
VP-WHT	Cessna 172F	53251	November 1977	A2-RBA, 9J-RBA, N5631R. C. W. Ferneyhough. Privately owned. (PRAW Rod Bater). Induna Bulawayo
VP-WHW	Cessna 185A Skywagon	0317	1978	EL-ADH (2), N4117Y. B. Nell – Fort Victoria (PRAW Barry Nel)
VP-WIA	Cessna U.206F Stationair	2581	1978	TL-AAT, M1357V. R. G. Pascoe, Rutherdale Farm – Shamva
VP-WIF	Reims-Cessna FR.172J Rocket	0375	December 1972	with A. C. Libreville, Gabon as TR-LRC, VP-WIF to R.C. Du Coudray & H. C. Sauzier (PRAW – Neville Pritchard)
VP-WIL	Cessna TU.206F Turbo Stationair	02288	Jan79	ZS-WHW, (N1927U). C. L. Bickle (1979) - Induna Bulawayo
VP-WIM	Reims-Cessna FR.172G Rocket	0215	1979	TR-LPA. K. L. Crowley Chiredzi
VP-WIN	PA-30 Twin Comanche B	30-1153	April 1976	ZS-EOU, N8061Y. D. A. Watt & M. H. Garde – Induna Bulawayo
VP-WIT	PA-28R-200 Cherokee Arrow	35107	January 1980	ZS-LMS, ZS-OMP, ZS-OMB, ZS-FWL. D. W. Howard (1980) - Umtali
VP-WIV	Cessna 182P Skylane	63069	December 1979	TR-LSH, N7282N. W. H. Barton (1979). Mount Darwin
VP-WIZ	Cessna 182L Skylane	59037	May 1977	ZS-FIR (w/o), N42846. A. I. Kluckow – Sinoia
VP-WJX	Cessna 180	31355		ZS-DKN, VP-YSU, ZS-DKN, N9256C. J. L. Potgieter (1980 post Zimbabwe Indep), P.J. Du Toit & A. J. Kriel. Mangula
VP-WKX	PA-23 Aztec 250E	27-4688		TR-LPQ, N14090. Techair (Pvt) Ltd (1980), to Norvall Brothers
VP-WLI	Piper PA-28-181 Archer II	7690106		N8220C, ZS-JUA (1976), later Z-WLI, then ZS-JUA
VP-WLU	Cessna 180J	52582		N9927N. N. R. Phillips (1981) Karoi
VP-WML	Cessna 310P	223		ZS-BBK, ZS-IAB, N5923M. P. S. Grobler (1982)
VP-WUG	Rand KR-2			C.R. Puzey (post 1982)
VP-YBL(2)	PA-28-180B Cherokee	1052	April 1963	ZS-CBL Risco & District Flying Club (PRAW Rod Bater)
VP-YDL(2)	Cessna 210			Owned by Executive Air (Peter James PRAW) when Rod Bater flew it on 9 February 1980, when on a training flight with Peter James
VP-YEF(2)	Cessna 150			Mashonaland Flying Club. Rod Bater flew this aircraft on PRAW training with the Midlands Flight Commander Tony Brown on the 13 July 1979. The aircraft was run by the Risco Flying Club. Rod used it extensively to teach students for the Risco Flying Club – he was an Instructor for the Club.
VP-YFX	Auster J/2 Arrow	2353	September 1947	New aircraft to RAMS, to Field Aircraft Services Ltd, Salisbury, to J. M. H. Lynch, Dawsons to J. M. H. Lynch, Newlands to Dixon & Yarwood Ltd, Salisbury, to P. H. Joscelyne, Bromley, January 1955 DBR in hangar collapse at Livingstone July 1956 to J. L. Manning, Sinoia (possible PRAW)
VP-YGA	Auster J/1 Autocrat	2196	September 1947	New aircraft to RAMS, to P. Fick, Marandellas, to I. C. McCran-Campbell, to H. Knill, Marandellas January 1958 A.D. Lawton, Umtali PRAW

Reg	Aircraft Type	C/N	Reg Date	Notes: Previous Registrations, Owner, Location (*continued*)
VP-YGZ	Beech 35 Bonanza	D-202	September 1947	ZS-BPR; 1 September 1947reg VP-YGZ to G. R. Smart, Rusape, pre 1 October 1960 to Andrews & Kidd Ltd, Salisbury, pre 1 Jul 1963 to W. G. Andrews, Salisbury March 1975 at Charles Prince The first aircraft to operate as Copper 159 and used to experiment with radios to evaluate suitability and compatibility with ground units. It was present at the 11–13 May 1962 training weekend. Later it took part and completed the World Vintage Air Rally from London to Sydney in 1990 as Z-YGZ https://abpic.co.uk/pictures/view/1017911
VP-YHL	Pipe-J-3C-65 Cub	21051	1947	NC2258M, Salisbury Aero Club, sold as VP-NAL, restored as VP-YHL, w/o 1965, canx
VP-YIS(2)	Rheims/Cessna FR.172FRocket	0106	1972	G-AWYK, Mashonaland Flying Club (PRAW Rod Bater) - Charles Prince
VP-YJA(2)	Cessna 180A	50199	1967	7Q-YTA E Gray, to J. W. Aitken Umtali to E. R. Harrison Chiredzi
VP-YJF	Auster J/5F Aiglet Trainer	2778	July 1952	G. H. Barry to E. M. Micklem, sold as ZS-HOS w/o 1983
VP-YJG(2)	Auster J/1 Autocrat	2200	June 1952	ZS-DBN to W. J. Ludgater, Bindura was present at 11–13 May 1962 training weekend, c.1968/9 to G. L. Roberts, Salisbury, pre March 1975 to L. F. Roberts, Induna, February 1976 sold to York Panelbeaters, George, SA as ZS-JPY
VP-YJX	Auster A.O.P.5	2051	September 1952	Copper 7, 65, 115, 31 – VP-KID, G-AWKH, TW507, H. Vogt. In 1960 H. C. Thorne of Ruwa to R. I. Lang of Ruwa 1962, to Aero Club of Matabeleland, to Peter Scales. 1964 Ian de la Rue, May 1967 to Friedrich Wolf of Umtali, who flew her regularly until 1971. Wolf applied to join PRAW but was refused because of his age, he handed the aircraft to son-in-law Peter Bell, on condition that it was used for PRAW duties. Peter had been a PRAW. Observer since 1962. Mrewa
VP-YJY	Luscombe 8E Silvaire	5190	September 1952	Previously in SA as ZS-BWJ, September 1952 regd VP-YJY to T. C. Woodforde, Salisbury (TAL October 1957) pre 1 July 1963 to M. A. Knight, Bulawayo, pre October 1965 to P. F. Scales, Bulawayo, July 1975 sold to K. P. Pearman, Baragwanath, SA as ZS-JKW
VP-YKA[2]	PA-32-300 Cherokee Six	40146	1973	9J-RGF TV Sales & Hire. (PRAW, James Barker) to M. Fowler
VP-YKB(2)	Cessna 182		March 1975	Previous Identity unknown, reg VP-YKB to P. C. Johnson March 197 at Charles Prince. On BASP Nominal Roll of Aircraft, 1 March 1974
VP-YKD	PA-28-235 Cherokee	10178	1966	Previously with J. D. Laubscher, Chingola, NR as 9J-RCD. Post April 1966 regd VP-YKD to R. M. & L. A. Westo Mashonaland flying Club – Bob Needham (PRAW)
VP-YLE	PA-22-135 Tri-Pacer	2077	July 1954	N3247B YLE to Air Carriers Ltd, Bulawayo to Victoria Falls Airways, Victoria Falls to Zambesi River Transport Service, Livingstone, to H. V. Chisnall, Mtokopost October 1965 to Tengwe Tri-Pacer Association (Brain van Buuren, Rupert Hildebrand, Dave Wiggens)
VP-YNR	Auster J/5	2878	January 1956	SR-54, RRAF54, W. Springer to H. B. Wiggins, Que Que, to R. J. Pendlebury, Kariba February 1966 sold to J. T. Coppock, Zambia as 9J-RBJ
VP-YNS	Auster J/5	2881	January 1956	RRAF56, to J. Rau, Salisbury, July 1957 to M. Simpson, Salisbury (PRAW) February 1960 sold to W. C. Landman, Empangeni, SA as ZS-CNS
VP-YOT[2]	Cessna 210D	58431	January 1972	ZS-DTT, N3931Y, To N Payne to A. Murray- Charles Prince
VP-YOW	PA-22 Tri-pacer 150	4251	January 1957	Field Engineering Ltd, Salisbury, H. Fick, Inyazura to Mashonaland Flying Club, Mount Hampden October 1965 to J. V. E. Wilson, Tjolotjo. Canx

Reg	Aircraft Type	C/N	Reg Date	**Notes: Previous Registrations, Owner, Location** (*continued*)
VP-YPI	DH.82A Tiger Moth	82260	April 1957	ZS-BVV (1947-57), SAAF 502, N9141. Built by de Havilland at Hatfield in August 1938. Delivered initially to 27 MU Shawbury for storage 15 August 1939 and then to 36MU Sealand 17 December 1939 for packing and dispatch to South Africa. Sold formally to the SAAF 19 January 1940 it became SAAF 502 and was sold for civilian use probably in 1946. Registered ZS-BVV, it was known to be with Rand Flying Club, Rand by 1954. Registered June 1955 to E. Yeld, Mtubatuba. Registration cancelled 24 April 1957. Regd in Rhodesia as VP-YPI 4.57 to J. G. Park, Bulawayo, to P. F. Scales, Bulawayo to R. J. Deane, Blantyre, fate not known.
VP-YPO	Auster J/5F Aiglet Trainer	AUS/191FM	September 1957	Built locally from spares September 1957 to G. L. Roberts, Mount Hampden, to W.R. Armstrong, Inyanga pre October 1965 to G. Lloyd-Roberts, Salisbury, post March 1975 canx NFK
VP-YPZ	PA-22-160 Tri-pacer 160	6031	March 1958	T. G. Voster (Construction) Ltd, Salisbury to Commoner Gold Mines Ltd, Salisbury pre October 1965 to Bensusan, Sharpe & Ashworth, Salisbury. (PRAW; Arthur Bensusan) July 1966 sold to Delkins Ltd, Zambia as 9J-RCP
VP-YRB	Luscombe 8E Silvaire	5265	September 1958	Registered new as N11B for export, ZS-BWC May 1959 to VP-YRB to W Murray-Smith Bulawayo 1961 to Katanga Air Force, 1963 WFU
VP-YRD	Beech K35 Bonanza	D-6006	March 1959	Reg VP-YRD to Lesbury Estate Ltd, Rusape post October 1975 to N. T. Waller. Was present at 11–13 May 1962 training weekend
VP-YRP	Cessna 180			On BASP Nominal Roll of Aircraft 1 March 1974
VP-YRS(2)	PA-32-260 Cherokee Six	248	July 1971	ZS-ELE, R. Anderson and Solly Benatar to Techair Ltd, crashed by Geoff York, John Plant of Techairre built it. Mount Hampden
VP-YRV	PA-20-135 Pacer	354	October 1965	ZS-DEL[1] post October 1960 regd VP-YRV to T. B. Bertleson, Salima, Ny, post July 1963 sold in Malawi as 7Q-YRV pre October 1965 regd VP-YRV to J. W. Aitken, Bindura then to Tem-Van syndicate
VP-YSE	Cessna 172B	47976	October 1960	N7476X, Mashonaland Flying Club (1960), Charles Prince
VP-YSL(2)	Cessna 172	29060	1966	Previously in Zambia as 9J-RCU, regd VP-YSL to R. M. Stirrup & Ptnron. BASP Nominal Roll of Aircraft, 1 March 1974
VP-YTC	Cessna 182B	51149	July 1963	Previously in the United States as N5049D, pre 1 July 1963 to Tobacco Advisory & Development Co Ltd, Salisbury, pre October 1965 to J. J. C. M. Lungen, Salisbury? to F. B. Johnson, March 1975 at Charles Prince. BASP Nominal Roll of Aircraft, 1 March 1974
VP-YTD	Cessna 210A	57727	July 1963	T. G. Voster (Construction) Ltd, Salisbury to Commoner Gold Mines Ltd, Salisbury October 1965to Bensusan, Sharpe & Ashworth, Salisbury. (PRAW Arthur Bensusan) July 1966 , sold to Delkins Ltd, Zambia as 9J-RCP. See VP-WCS
VP-YTG	Cessna 172B	47751	1961	Previously in SA as ZS-COF, regd VP-YTG owner unknown pre 1 July 1963 to African Air Charters Ltd, Ndola, NR, pre October 1965 to RUAC, Salisbury, 1965, reg in Zambia as VP-RTG? regd VP-YTG to Henderson & Sons Ltd, Induna pre March 1975 to Skywork, Charles Prince 18 April 1980 at Induna, on BASP Nominal Roll of Aircraft, 1 March 1974
VP-YTV	Cessna 180	32089		ZS-DNN, N3291D, to Aero Services (Rhodesia) Ltd, Salisbury E. D. Strever to Tango Victor Syndicate. (PRAW Bill Ludgater) Bindura
VP-YUB	PA-28-160 Cherokee	294	January 1962	N11C R. E. Davenport, Salisbury, sold to C. W. Landrey, Virginia, SA as ZS-CZS
VP-YUG	Cessna 172C	49301	June 1962	ZS-CUV, N1601Y, W. A. R. MacDonald (PRAW) to P. G. Fargnoli Bulawayo

Reg	Aircraft Type	C/N	Reg Date	Notes: Previous Registrations, Owner, Location (*continued*)
VP-YUI	Beech A35 Bonanza	D-1940	May 1962	ZS-DAM (1949-62), Alfred 'Denty' Lawton, Canx
VP-YUJ	Cessna 182A	51525	1962	W. D. Burton, to Ernie Berk (PRAW), to Pip C. M. Thornycroft September 1981. Also owned at some stage by Mashonaland Flying Club. PRAW Rod Baterflew this aircraft on PRAW with 2 pax on both 18 and 19 April 1980.
VP-YUW	Cessna 172D	49942	December 1962	N2342U to BDS Syndicate, Mount Hampden to Skywork Ltd, Salisbury to Barbour, Dryden & Standish-White, Salisbury, to Eastern Gateway Air Services (Peter Marchussen PRAW) Lomagundi
VP-YUY	PA-22-135 Tri-Pacer	2106	January 1963	ZS-DJW, VQ-ZIC, ZS-DJW, P. Brittlebank & Co (Pvt.) Ltd to P. G. Coetse, for sale as ZS-LCX in 1981. Owned by R.A. Stigling of Somerset West from 1994
VP-YVE	Cessna 172	50176		N2576U to Siyalisa Estates Ltd, to M. B. McGrath, Salisbury
VP-YVG	PA-18A Super Cub 150	7942		J. S. Ball, (PRAW) sold as ZS-FRL in 1969, restored to Sby Gliding Club Warren Hills
VP-YVH	PA-28-160 Cherokee	28-55	April 1963	Previously in SA as ZS-CUD, April 1963 reg VP-YVH to H. Ferreira, Sinoia, on BASP Nominal Roll of Aircraft of 1 March 1974
VP-YVL	Cessna 172D	50455	June 1963	N2855U, R. G. Pascoe (PRAW) to Mr & Mrs C. H. Stijkel
VP-YWA(2)	Cessna 210H	59006	1977	9J-RIB, ZS-FFV, N6106F, J. B. Connor (PRAW) and T. C. Connor 1977, Chipinga
VP-YWB(2)	Cessna 172H	55824	January 1967	7Q-YFD to E. Parker, Mount Hampden July 1973 E. Parker, Charles Prince, post October 1975 to W. J. Watson of Tengwe
VP-YWD	PA-28-180 Cherokee B	1135	September 1963	ZS-CBM, M. Anthony 1963, canx Bindura
VP-YWH	Cessna 172E	50725	October 1963	N3525S to B. C. W. Hacking, Karoi
VP-YWI	Cessna 182	33629	October 1963	ZS-CEC (1956-63), N5629B, later Z-YWI, ZS-PGF (2004). Chipinga Garages (Pvt) Ltd, to T. H. MacMillan & W. O. Stetter
VP-YWL(2)	Cessna 180F	51268	March 1971	N2168Z to W. J. Ludgater, Bindura. (PRAW; Bill Ludgater) Crashed 5 December 80, 4 killed inc Phillipa Berlyn
VP-YXF	Mooney M20C	2783	July 1964	X-ray Foxtrot Syndicate (Allan Abrey), Mount Hampden to D. T. Saunders (accident taking off from a grass strip in Gwelo). July 73 to Dr J.D. Burrows, Mount Hampden then Charles Prince (TAL March 1975)
VP-YXI	PA-28-180B Cherokee	1714	May 1964	New Aircraft reg to Piper Aircraft as N11C – for export, reg VP-YXI to S. Nielsen, Bindura post October 1975 to F. Hassbrook, on BASP Nominal Roll of Aircraft, 1 March 1974
VP-YXO	Mooney M.20E	521	November 1964	N79858, Dr. J.D. Burrows (1964) to J. S. Brown (PRAW Strath Brown). Darwendale/Charles Prince
VP-YXP	Mooney M.20F Executive	670335	August 1970	ZS-EUG (1) 1966, later Z-YXP, ZS-PBX (2003), Mashonaland Flying Club [1970]
VP-YXT	PA-28-180C Cherokee	1832	January 1965	ZS-DZV Techair Ltd, Salisbury to C. R. Horsley (PRAW Mike Gardner)
VP-YXV	Cessna 182F Skylane	54893	December 1964	Previously with Campling Bros & Vanderval Ltd, Kenya as VP-KSZ, reg VP-YXV to Norman, Evans, Batstone & Costerveen, Salisbury post August 1970, reg in Malawi as 7Q-YDV, pre February 1974 reg VP-YXV to P. R. & J. J. Maude, on BASP Nominal Roll of Aircraft 1 March 1974
VP-YXW	PA-28 Cherokee 180C	2082		N11C, M. J. Dawson Shamva
VP-YXY	Cessna 182B	51004	1965	Previously in Mozambique as CR-AFX, reg VP-YXY to C. B. Davy, Fort Victoria, post October 1975 to K. J. Grant PRAW, on BASP Nominal Roll of Aircraft of 1 March 1974
VP-YXZ	Cessna 182H	56322	May 1965	N2422X W H Barton 1 September 1978 VP-YXZ was riddled with bullets and set alight in Barton's hangar,

Reg	Aircraft Type	C/N	Reg Date	Notes: Previous Registrations, Owner, Location (*continued*)
VP-YYA	Cessna 206	0261	1965	N5261U Dept of Civil Aviation (1978–9 PRAW Gerry Cleveland)
VP-YYB	Cessna U.206	0352	1965	N2152F, Skywork (pvt) Ltd (1965), to District Development Fund, w/o 19 February 1979
VP-YYE	PA-28-235 Cherokee	10568	1965	New Aircraft -reg to Piper Aircraft as N11C. for export, reg VP-YYE to L. Van Rooyen, Triangle, post October 1965 to T. I. F. Sandeman, on BASP Nominal Roll of Aircraft 1 March 1974
VP-YYF	PA-28-180 Cherokee C	2100	1965	N11C C F Haasbroek Umvukwes
VP-YYK	Cessna 310 (Riley 65)	35044	1965	G-ARTK (Keegan Aviation 1963), N2644C. RUAC (1965) to E. H. Smit. Also owned by Peter Scales, Bulawayo
VP-YYL	PA-24-260B Comanche	4151	1965	ZS-EBU. To H Dax
VP-YYO	Cessna 180	31834	1965	N9436C, later ZS-YYO (1971) later canx, T. N. Coutney (1965)
VP-YYT	Cessna 172	36416	August 1965	ZS-CHD, N8716B, O. H. Knight and P. D. Hart (1965), to G. W. Heasman
ZS-DIT	Cessna U206E	01589	1972	S. A. Moorcroft as per PRAW contact list
ZS-DWK	Piper PA-28-235 Cherokee	210261		ZS-DWK, V5-DWK,ZS-DWK,A2-AAY,ZS-DWK (1964), N11C, N8726W – ZS-DWK later cancelled – returned to ZS-DWK 2010
ZS-EDM	Mooney M20C Mark 21	3360	1973	To Z-WNX February 1985 to Garry Douglas, Mutare PRAW owner and pilot John Tayler
ZS-EIG	Piper PA-23-250 Aztec			Techair, Charles Prince PRAW pilot Mike Gardner
ZS-EOT	Piper PA-28 Cherokee			Techair, Charles Prince PRAW pilot Mike Gardner
ZS-EVI	Piper PA32 Cherokee 300C			Techair, Charles Prince PRAW pilot Mike Gardner
ZS-EWD	Cessna 210 Centurion			RUAC PRAW Cleveland and M. Anthony. Several ZS registrations only appear on an original PRAW contact list. They are not on an available South African register
ZS-EWH	Cessna 182			PRAW C. R. Puzey as per PRAW contact list
ZS-EZZ	Cessna 182			PRAW H. P. Raynor as per PRAW contact list
ZS-FCU	Cessna 182-L	58629	1968	N3329, March 1968 ZS-FCU, owned in Rhodesia by Ernie Parker as FCU, written off at Henneman 21 July 1992, owned by Dr F. J. Delport.
ZS-FVL	PA-32-300C Cherokee	40621		ZS-FVL (current), Z-WPU, ZS-FVL (1969), N4263R. Owned in Rhodesia by Roy Anderson, Owned by Salto Trading (One) CC of Bronkhorstspruit in 2004
ZS-GBC	Beech E33C Bonanza	CJ-24	1975	ZS-GBC was originally an E33A serial CE-263 that was converted to an E33C serial CJ-24. Only 25 E33C these aerobatic versions were built. The registration is the initials of the then owner Graeme Brian Conlyn – GBC. PRAW Mike Simpson, Bulawayo https://www.flickr.com/photos/23199966@N02/49394515801/in/photolist-2ifPNEM
ZS-GBL	Cessna U 206		1977	Matabeleland Flying School PRAW Bob Needham, to Mike Coley of Coley Hall Transport February 1980
ZS-IFD	Cessna 310P	0099		Operated by Cane Air in Rhodesia/Zimbabwe as ZS-IFD (1970 to 1986), later regd Z-WPS, previously 9J-AAC, N5799M
ZS-IOF	Cessna 182			PRAW C. H. Wilcox as per PRAW contact list
ZS-IUX	Cessna 182P Skylane	61573	October 1978	W. H. Barton wrote in the The Outpost 1 December 1979 that VP-WIV replaced ZS-IUX note that prior to the arrival WIV he flew as an observer for Bundu Waller
ZS-IYG	Cessna 207			BASP Nominal Roll of Aircraft 1 March 1974

Reg	Aircraft Type	C/N	Reg Date	Notes: Previous Registrations, Owner, Location (*continued*)
ZS-IYN	Cessna U.206F	03007		Previously N2884Q, regd ZS-IYN in 1975 (cancelled 1984), exported as Z-WNK. SALOPS Wing (T. Mann)
ZS-IWN	Cessna 182P	64290	1996	PRAW D. P. Mulock-Bentley as per PRAW contact list
ZS-IWW	Cessna P.206D	0523	1975	1969,Twin City Development (Pty) Ltd
ZS-JIL	PA-32-300 Cherokee Six C	40952	April 1975	Acquired by Allan Abrey in 1974, used for PRAW duties. Noted for sale in South Africa in 2001 for R460 000. Originally N8983N (3 August 1970), then ZS-JIL (April 1975 to 21 March 1985), 3D-ADU (Swaziland) (21 March 1985 to 4 August 1992), ZS-JIL 4 August 1992 to date)
ZS-JKX	Cessna 185 Float Plane			Peter Anderson, Kariba
ZS-JUM	Cessna T.210K Turbo Centurion	9330 or 03007	February 1976	Brian van Buuren, Umtali, painted anti-strella grey. Became Z-BVB. Not owned by Mrs C. A. Hosking of Fishhoek in 1979
ZS-JVK	Cessna 336	0053		Previously A2-ZEZ,A2-BGI,A2-ZEZ,XB-SIV,N1753Z. Owned by Peter Scales as A2-ZEZ in Bulawayo. ZS-JVK 1976–96, went missing between East London and Pietermaritzburg – presumed lost at sea. 22 February 1996
JS-JWK	Piper Aztec			Owned by Allan Abrey and Dr 'Mike' Standish-White
ZS-KBG	Cessna 206			PRAW G W Donald as per PRAW contact list
ZS-ZGZ	Cessna 206	01003	1974	Previously A2-ZGZ,5Y-AHG. Regd ZS-ZGZ in 1974. Later VP-WPZ, Z-WPZ, ZS-OCF (1997), ZS-ZGZ (2nd time). used by SALOPS wing as ZS-ZGZ in the late 1970s (T. Mann)

Appendix III
PRAW Awards & Decorations

Complied by Paul Brewster

Name	Rank	Number	Date	Award Source & Date
	Member of the Order of British Empire			
Smart, G. R.	PRP	4031	01/01/63	Supplement to The London Gazette, 28 December 1962, Issue 42870
Springer, W. J.	Major	3480G	12/06/65	Supplement to The London Gazette, 4 Jun 1965, Issue 43667
	Commendation			
Brittlebank, P.	PRP	14240Z	1967	BSAP Annual Report 1967, p.13
Barnett, V.	PRO	14559Z	1967	BSAP Annual Report 1967, p.13
	Citation: Two members of the Air Wing were awarded commendations by the Commissioner in recognition of the high standard of efficiency, great skill and tenacity of purpose displayed by them during operations against terrorists in Matabeleland. The PRAW crew along with two RhAF Provosts dived down on the 'Lobegula Group' of insurgents, to distract them as ground forces recovered several wounded police and RAR.			
Brown	PRP	7376	1962	1962 BSAP Annual Report 1962 & FO 217/62
MacDonald, W. A. R.	PRP	5145R	1971	BSAP Annual Report 1971, p.10. (no citation found)

Name	Rank	Number	Date	Award Source & Date (*continued*)
Magee, J. H.	PRP	6998F	1962	BSAP Annual Report 1962 & FO 217/62
	Legion of Merit – Member (Civilian)			
Ludgater, W. J.	PRP	6282C	17/06/71	RN 1117/71 The Rhodesia Government Gazette – Extraordinary, 12 July 1971, Vol.XLIX, No.32, Page 829
	Legion of Merit – Member (Military)			
Palmer, P. P.	PRP	7006P	07/11/79	RN 1259/79 The Zimbabwe Rhodesia Government Gazette, 7 December 1979, Vol.LVII, No.70, Page 1043
	Meritorious Conduct Medal			
Knight O. H.	PRP	13747E	19/11/79	RN1259/79 The Zimbabwe Rhodesia Government Gazette, 7 December 1979, Vol.LVII, No.70, Page 1043
Watson J. R.	PRP	27065S	19/11/79	RN1259/79 The Zimbabwe Rhodesia Government Gazette, 7 December 1979, Vol.LVII, No.70, Page 1043
	Meritorious Conduct Medal (Military)			
Anderson, R. L.	PRP	15099L	14/11/78	RN 1280/78 The Rhodesia Government Gazette – Extraordinary, 11 November 1978, Vol.LVI, No.60, Page 1030
Barton, W. H.	PRP	12274Q	14/11/78	RN 1280/78 The Rhodesia Government Gazette – Extraordinary, 11 November 1978, Vol.LVI, No.60, Page 1030
Bickle, C. L.	PRP	12186V	14/11/78	RN 1280/78 The Rhodesia Government Gazette – Extraordinary, 11 November 1978, Vol.LVI, No.60, Page 1030
Boltt, C. R.	PRP	5791T	14/10/75	RN 1534A/75 The Rhodesia Government Gazette – Extraordinary, 11 November 1976, Vol.LIV, No.57, Page 1237
Browne, V. A. D.	PRP	9022F	29/09/76	RN 1279/76 The Rhodesia Government Gazette – Extraordinary, 11 November 1976, Vol.LIV, No.57, Page 1237
Chisnall, H. V.	PRP	6110Q	11/10/77	RN 1202/77 The Rhodesia Government Gazette – Extraordinary, 11 November 1977, Vol.LV, No.57, Page 1004
Cleveland, G. M.	PRP	9151W	20/11/79	RN 1259/79 The Zimbabwe Rhodesia Government Gazette, 7 December 1979, Vol.LVII, No.70, Page 1044
Cowan, H.	PRP	11103S	14/10/75	RN 1534A/75 The Rhodesia Government Gazette, 11 November 1975, Vol.LIII, No.52, Page 1312
Dax, H. F.	PRP	4735W	14/10/78	RN 1280/78 The Rhodesia Government Gazette – Extraordinary, 11 November 1978, Vol.LVI, No.60, Page 1030
Garde, M. H.	PRP	17061T	14/10/78	RN 1280/78 The Rhodesia Government Gazette – Extraordinary, 11 November 1978, Vol.LVI, No.60, Page 1030
Honman, J. O.	PRP	15336T	20/03/79	RN 437/79 The Rhodesia Government Gazette, 13 April 1979, Vol.LVII, No.24, Page 328
Howard, D. W.	PRP	19804A	11/10/77	RN 1202/77 The Rhodesia Government Gazette – Extraordinary, 11 November 1977, Vol.LV, No.57, Page 1004
Jellicoe, L. M.	PRP	14681G	14/10/78	RN 1280/78 The Rhodesia Government Gazette – Extraordinary, 11 November 1978, Vol.LVI, No.60, Page 1030
Manning, J. L.	PRP	6380J	14/10/78	RN 1280/78 The Rhodesia Government Gazette – Extraordinary, 11 November 1978, Vol.LVI, No.60, Page 1030
Palmer, P. P.	PRP	7006P	14/10/75	RN 1534A/75 The Rhodesia Government Gazette, 11 November 1975, Vol.LIII, No.52, Page 1312
Parker, E.	PRP	8324X	20/11/79	RN 1259/79 The Zimbabwe Rhodesia Government Gazette, 7 December 1979, Vol.LVII, No.70, Page 1044
Plant, J. F.	PRP	15333Q	20/11/79	RN 1259/79 The Zimbabwe Rhodesia Government Gazette, 7 December 1979, Vol.LVII, No.70, Page 1044
Style, R. E.	PRP	8899X	14/10/78	RN 1280/78 The Rhodesia Government Gazette – Extraordinary, 11 November 1978, Vol.LVI, No.60, Page 1030
van Buuren, B. A.	PRP	9047H	14/10/78	RN 1280/78 The Rhodesia Government Gazette – Extraordinary, 11 November 1978, Vol.LVI, No.60, Page 1030
Waller, N. T.	PRP	12296P	14/10/78	RN 1280/78 The Rhodesia Government Gazette – Extraordinary, 11 November 1978, Vol.LVI, No.60, Page 1030
	Commissioners Commendations Commissioners Special Commendation (CSC – Silver Baton) Commissioners Commendation (CC – Bronze Baton)			

Name	Rank	Number	Date	Award Source & Date (*continued*)
Boltt, C.R.	PRP	5791T	1974	FO 114/74 CSC – Silver Baton
Wilcox, C. H.	PRP	8501P	1978	FO 279/78 CSC – Silver Baton
Citation	No. 8501, Police Reserve Pilot WILCOX In recognition of the professional ability, determination and devotion to duty displayed by him on 11 July 1978 whilst providing aerial cover for the Kariba to Karoi convoy. During a terrorist ambush on the convoy, Police Reserve Pilot WILCOX identified the terrorist' position and dived on this position in his unarmed aircraft on two occasions. On the second occasion he was subjected to enemy fire and his aircraft hit. Thereafter he flew low over the convoy and dropped a medical pack to assist ground forces in attending the injured. The actions of Police Reserve Pilot WILCOX assisted in quickly terminating what was a determined terrorist attack. Police Reserve Pilot WILCOX is granted the right to wear the insignia of the Silver Baton.			
Barnett, C.	PRO	14599Z	1974	FO 114/74 Bronze Baton
Dax, H. F.	PRP	4735W	1976	FO 111/76 Bronze Baton
Haasbroek, C. F.	PRP	11473V	1976	FO 111/76 Bronze Baton
Citation	No. 4735W. Police Reserve Pilot DAX, H. F. No. 11473V, Police Reserve Pilot HAASBROEK. C.F. who, during the course of exacting duties in the operational area on Friday, 6 February 1976, displayed a high degree of professional ability, initiative, determination and mental endurance beyond the normal call of duty. Police Reserve Pilot Dax and Police Reserve Pilot Haasbroek are granted the right to wear the insignia of the Bronze Baton.			
Postlethwayt, C. W. G.	PRP	15923G	1978	FO 193/78 Bronze Baton
Citation	No. 15923, Police Reserve Pilot POSTLETHWAITE in recognition of the professional ability and devotion to duty displayed by him during the crash landing of a Police Reserve Air Wing aircraft on 30 March, 1978 in the Operation Hurricane area. The aircraft suffered a fractured oil pipeline and oil covered the aircraft windscreen thus hindering the pilot's field of vision. In spite of this. Police Reserve Pilot POSTLETHWAITE remained calm and was able to crash land the aircraft. Police Reserve Pilot POSTLETHWAITE is hereby granted the right to wear the insignia of the Bronze Baton.			
	Rhodesia General Service Medal (RhGSM) Police Reserve Air Wing			
Abrey, A. N. S.	PRP	21988Z	29/12/1977	PGHQ, PRAW, Suppl to BSAP R FO, 24th Sched, 29 December 1977, p.3
Adams, John Peter	PRO	3812S	08/01/1970	PRAW, Suppl to BSAP R FO, 1st Sched, 8 January 1970, p.1
Addison, A. C.	PRP	22589C	29/12/1977	PGHQ, PRAW, Suppl to BSAP R FO, 24th Sched, 29 December 1977, p.3
Addison, D. C.	PRP	14374Y	29/12/1977	PGHQ, PRAW, Suppl to BSAP R FO, 24th Sched, 29 December 1977, p.3
Aitken, J. W. 'Jimmy'	PRP	10097Z	11/12/1975	Man Prov, PRAW, Suppl to BSAP R FO, 18th Sched, 11 December 1975, p.2
Alford, Alan Michael	PRP	3626Q	08/05/1975	Mash Prov, PRAW, Suppl to BSAP R FO, 15th Sched, 8 May 1975, p.2
Anderson, Roy Leslie	PRP	15099L	29/05/1975	Sby Prov, PRAW, Suppl to BSAP R FO, 16th Sched, 29 May 1975, p.2
Anthony, Michael 'Micky'	PRP	8806W	29/12/1977	Mash Prov, PRAW, Suppl to BSAP R FO, 24th Sched, 29 December 1977, p.1
Ashworth, Michael G. 'Mike'	PRP	14188W	29/05/1975	Sby Prov, PRAW, Suppl to BSAP R FO, 16th Sched, 29 May 1975, p.1

Name	Rank	Number	Date	Award Source & Date (*continued*)
Austin, L . S.	PRO	17846X	11/12/1975	Mat Prov, PRAW, Suppl to BSAP R FO, 18th Sched, 11 December 1975, p.5
Ball, J. S.	PRP	10395Y	11/12/1975	Man Prov, PRAW, Suppl to BSAP R FO, 18th Sched, 11 December 1975, p.2
Barnett, Cecil	PRP	14559Z	08/01/1970	PRAW, Suppl to BSAP R FO, 1st Sched, 8 January 1970, p.1
Barton, Walter Hutcheons 'Wally'	PRP	12274Q	29/12/1977	Mash Prov, PRAW, Suppl to BSAP R FO, 24th Sched, 29 December 1977, p.1
Bater, R. W. I. 'Rod'	PRP	24632Y	20/12/1979	Mid Prov, PRAW, Suppl to BSAP R FO, 55th Sched, 20 December 1979, p.5
Bell, G. M. B.	PRO	11500Z	29/12/1977	Mash Prov, PRAW, Suppl to BSAP R FO, 24th Sched, 29 December 1977, p.1
Bell, Peter R.	PRO	3463N	10/10/1974	Mash Prov, PRAW, Suppl to BSAP R FO, 14th Sched, 10 October 1974, p.1
Beniston, J. M.	PRO	15277E	20/12/1979	Mash Prov, PRAW, Suppl to BSAP R FO, 55th Sched, 20 December 1979, p.2
Benjamin, H. J.	PRP	29194G	01/05/1981	Sby Prov, PRAW, Suppl to BSAP R FO, 64th Sched, undated, p.4
Berk, E. R.	PRP	380149E	01/05/1981	Sby Prov, PRAW, Suppl to BSAP R FO, 64th Sched, undated, p.4
Bickle, Colin Lancaster	PRP	12186V	08/01/1970	PRAW, Suppl to BSAP R FO, 1st Sched, 8 January 1970, p.1
Boltt, Charles Richard 'Dicky'	PRP	5791T	05/02/1970	PRAW, Suppl to BSAP R FO, 3rd Sched, 5 February 1970, p.1
Bondi, I.	PRP	14228P	29/05/1975	Sby Prov, PRAW, Suppl to BSAP R FO, 16th Sched, 29 May 1975, p.1
Bradley, B. A. F.	PRP	15281J	03/03/1977	Sby Prov, PRAW, Suppl to BSAP R FO, 19th Sched, 3 March 1977, p.21
Bradshaw, Richard James	PRO	15118G	29/12/1977	Mat Prov, PRAW, Suppl to BSAP R FO, 24th Sched, 29 December 1977, p.2
Breeze, D. T.	PRO	16941N	29/12/1977	Mash Prov, PRAW, Suppl to BSAP R FO, 24th Sched, 29 December 1977, p.1
Brink, D. J.	PRP	19096F	29/12/1977	Mash Prov, PRAW, Suppl to BSAP R FO, 24th Sched, 29 December 1977, p.2
Brittlebank, Percy Philip 'Phil'	PRP	14240C	08/01/1970	PRAW, Suppl to BSAP R FO, 1st Sched, 8 January 1970, p.1
Brown, J. S.	PRO	14326W	01/05/1981	Mash Prov, PRAW, Suppl to BSAP R FO, 63rd Sched, undated, p.2
Brown, R. C.	PRP	16827P	29/12/1977	PGHQ, PRAW, Suppl to BSAP R FO, 24th Sched, 29 December 1977, p.3
Brown, Strath B.	PRO	14760S	08/05/1975	Mash Prov, PRAW, Suppl to BSAP R FO, 15th Sched, 8 May 1975, p.3
Browne, Vernon Anthony Dennison 'Tony'	PRP	9022F	17/01/1974	Mid Prov, PRAW, Suppl to BSAP R FO, 13th Sched, 17 January 1974, p.2
Browning, M. W.	PRO	17490K	11/12/1975	Man Prov, PRAW, Suppl to BSAP R FO, 18th Sched, 11 December 1975, p.3
Burgess, P. M.	PRO	17277D	29/12/1977	Mash Prov, PRAW, Suppl to BSAP R FO, 24th Sched, 29 December 1977, p.1
Cartwright, C. D.	PRO	18769A	29/12/1977	Mash Prov, PRAW, Suppl to BSAP R FO, 24th Sched, 29 December 1977, p.2
Challoner, H..	PRP	18796E	29/12/1977	Mash Prov, PRAW, Suppl to BSAP R FO, 24th Sched, 29 December 1977, p.2
Chandler, B. R. H.	PRP	24517Y	29/12/1977	Mat Prov, PRAW, Suppl to BSAP R FO, 24th Sched, 29 December 1977, p.2
Cherry, Timothy Andrew 'Tim'	PRO	22303R	29/12/1977	Mash Prov, PRAW, Suppl to BSAP R FO, 24th Sched, 29 December 1977, p.2
Chisnall, Hugh V.	PRP	6110Q	10/10/1974	Mash Prov, PRAW, Suppl to BSAP R FO, 14th Sched, 10 October 1974, p.1
Church, P. F.	PRP	20931A	29/12/1977	Mash Prov, PRAW, Suppl to BSAP R FO, 24th Sched, 29 December 1977, p.2
Connor, John B.	PRP	20192X	11/12/1975	Man Prov, PRAW, Suppl to BSAP R FO, 18th Sched, 11 December 1975, p.4
Cowan, Henry	PRP	11103S	08/05/1975	Sby Prov, PRAW, Suppl to BSAP R FO, 15th Sched, 8 May 1975, p.11

Name	Rank	Number	Date	Award Source & Date (*continued*)
Danes, N. D.	PRP	26950S	01/05/1981	Sby Prov, PRAW, Suppl to BSAP R FO, 65th Sched, Undated, p.8
Darlow, R. G. E. 'Poogie'	PRP	21995G	29/12/1977	Mat Prov, PRAW, Suppl to BSAP R FO, 24th Sched, 29 December 1977, p.2
Davenport, R. E.	PRP	19180X	29/12/1977	PGHQ, PRAW, Suppl to BSAP R FO, 24th Sched, 29 December 1977, p.3
Davies, A. C.	PRP	23355K	29/12/1977	Vic Prov, PRAW, Suppl to BSAP R FO, 24th Sched, 29 December 1977, p.4
Dawson, Michael J. 'Mike'	PRP	7231J	29/12/1977	Man Prov, PRAW, Suppl to BSAP R FO, 24th Sched, 29 December 1977, p.1
Dax, Hamilton Fenner 'Hammy'	PRO	4735W	08/10/1970	Mash Prov, PRAW, Suppl to BSAP R FO, 24th Sched, 29 December 1977, p.1
de Jong, L. J.	PRO	13253E	29/12/1977	PRAW, Suppl to BSAP R FO, 6th Sched, 8 October 1970, p.1
Dean, R. B.	PRP	17955Q	29/12/1977	Mash Prov, PRAW, Suppl to BSAP R FO, 24th Sched, 29 December 1977, p.1
Dods-Brooks, S. H.	PRP	14918P	01/07/1979	Mash Prov, PRAW, Suppl to BSAP R FO, 24th Sched, 29 December 1977, p.2
Downey, L. P.	PRP	23347B	01/07/1979	Mash Prov, PRAW, Suppl to BSAP R FO, 48th Sched, Jul 1979, p.1
Fenner, R.	PRP	22564A	29/12/1977	Mash Prov, PRAW, Suppl to BSAP R FO, 49th Sched, Jul 1979, p.1
Fernandes, G. R. L. 'Bob'	PRP	23688X	29/12/1977	Mat Prov, PRAW, Suppl to BSAP R FO, 24th Sched, 29 December 1977, p.2
Foreman, G. K.	PRO	7625M	29/12/1977	Mat Prov, PRAW, Suppl to BSAP R FO, 24th Sched, 29 December 1977, p.2
Garde, Michael Henry 'Mike'	PRP	17061T	29/12/1977	Mid Prov, PRAW, Suppl to BSAP R FO, 24th Sched, 29 December 1977, p.2
Gibson, D. E.	PRO	7936A	11/12/1975	Mat Prov, PRAW, Suppl to BSAP R FO, 24th Sched, 29 December 1977, p.2
Gibson, G. D.	PRO	18733L	20/12/1979	Man Prov, PRAW, Suppl to BSAP R FO, 18th Sched, 11 December 1975, Pp.4
Graham, Allan Albert	PRP	14612G	08/01/1970	Mash Prov, PRAW, Suppl to BSAP R FO, 55th Sched, 20 December 1979, p.2
Graham-Owen, Lester James	PRP	10283B	26/02/1970	PRAW, Suppl to BSAP R FO, 1st Sched, 8 January 1970, p.1
Grant, Kenneth J. 'Ken'	PRP	21223S	29/12/1977	PRAW, Suppl to BSAP R FO, 4th Sched, 26 February 1970, p.1
Griffin, Milton Lionel	PRP	9391G	08/01/1970	Man Prov, PRAW, Suppl to BSAP R FO, 24th Sched, 29 December 1977, p.1
Grobler, P. S.	PRP	10587G	29/12/1977	PRAW, Suppl to BSAP R FO, 1st Sched, 8 January 1970, p.1
Grobler, S. P.	PRP	19780Z	24/02/1979	Mash Prov, PRAW, Suppl to BSAP R FO, 24th Sched, 29 December 1977, p.1
Hacking, Bertram Cecil William 'Bert'	PRP	9687D	08/01/1970	Mash Prov, PRAW, Suppl to BSAP R FO, 46th Sched, 24 February 1979, p.4
Hall, P. N.	PRP	23862L	29/12/1977	PRAW, Suppl to BSAP R FO, 1st Sched, 8 January 1970, p.1
Hart, P. D.	PRP	15226Z	08/05/1975	PGHQ, PRAW, Suppl to BSAP R FO, 24th Sched, 29 December 1977, p.3
Harty, D. P.	PRP	17780A	03/03/1977	Mat Prov, PRAW, Suppl to BSAP R FO, 15th Sched, 8 May 1975, p.6
Harvey, George James William 'Hamish'	PRP	20932B	29/12/1977	Mid Prov, PRAW, Suppl to BSAP R FO, 19th Sched, 3 March 1977, p.18
Henderson, I. M.	PRP	8523N	29/12/1977	Mash Prov, PRAW, Suppl to BSAP R FO, 24th Sched, 29 December 1977, p.2
Hildebrand, Rupert C.	PRO	16836Z	11/12/1975	Mat Prov, PRAW, Suppl to BSAP R FO, 24th Sched, 29 December 1977, p.2
Hole, E. D.	PRP	17398T	29/12/1977	Man Prov, PRAW, Suppl to BSAP R FO, 18th Sched, 11 December 1975, p.3
Howard, Donald W. 'Don'	PRP	19804A	11/12/1975	Mid Prov, PRAW, Suppl to BSAP R FO, 24th Sched, 29 December 1977, p.2
Howell, D. L. M.	PRP	6558C	11/12/1975	Man Prov, PRAW, Suppl to BSAP R FO, 18th Sched, 11 December 1975, p.3

Name	Rank	Number	Date	Award Source & Date (*continued*)
James, P. L.	PRP	21517M	29/12/1977	Man Prov, PRAW, Suppl to BSAP R FO, 18th Sched, 11 December 1975, p.1
Jameson, Derek Bruce	PRO	5014Z	29/12/1977	Mid Prov, PRAW, Suppl to BSAP R FO, 24th Sched, 29 December 1977, p.3
Jellicoe, Leslie Malcolm 'Les'	PRP	14681G	29/12/1977	Mid Prov, PRAW, Suppl to BSAP R FO, 24th Sched, 29 December 1977, p.2
Jones, G. M.	PRO	17395G	17/01/1974	Mash Prov, PRAW, Suppl to BSAP R FO, 24th Sched, 29 December 1977, p.1
Jordan, R. A.	PRP	15035R	29/12/1977	Mid Prov, PRAW, Suppl to BSAP R FO, 13th Sched, 17 January 1974, p.2
Keith, Brian Michael	PRO	20568F	29/12/1977	Mash Prov, PRAW, Suppl to BSAP R FO, 24th Sched, 29 December 1977, p.1
Knight, M. A.	PRP	17765J	29/12/1977	Man Prov, PRAW, Suppl to BSAP R FO, 24th Sched, 29 December 1977, p.1
Knight, O. H. 'Olly'	PRP	13747R	29/12/1977	Mat Prov, PRAW, Suppl to BSAP R FO, 24th Sched, 29 December 1977, p.2
Linfield, Gabriel William Roy 'Bill'	PRP	25829Z	01/07/1979	Mat Prov, PRAW, Suppl to BSAP R FO, 24th Sched, 29 December 1977, p.2
Ludgater, William John 'Bill'	PRP	6282C	26/02/1970	Mash Prov, PRAW, Suppl to BSAP R FO, 49th Sched, July 1979, p.1
Lyon, Douglas H. 'Dougie'	PRO	6477P	29/12/1977	PRAW, Suppl to BSAP R FO, 4th Sched, 26 February 1970, Pp.1
MacDonald, William Alistair Ross	PRP	5145R	05/02/1970	Mash Prov, PRAW, Suppl to BSAP R FO, 24th Sched, 29 December 1977, p.1
Magee, John Herbert	PRP	6998F	08/10/1970	PRAW, Suppl to BSAP R FO, 3rd Sched, 5 February 1970, p.1
Manning, Francis Lane	PRP	10112Q	05/02/1970	PRAW, Suppl to BSAP R FO, 6th Sched, 8 October 1970, p.1
Manning, John Lane	PRP	6380J	07/05/1970	PRAW, Suppl to BSAP R FO, 3rd Sched, 5 February 1970, p.1
Martin, A. C.	PRO	24747Y	29/12/1977	PRAW, Suppl to BSAP R FO, 5th Sched, 7 May 1970, Pg 1
Maurice, K. G.	PRP	21803Y	29/12/1977	Mash Prov, PRAW, Suppl to BSAP R FO, 24th Sched, 29 December 1977, p.2
Morton, H. J. W.	PRO	13805E	11/12/1975	PGHQ, PRAW, Suppl to BSAP R FO, 24th Sched, 29 December 1977, p.3
Needham, R. J. A.	PRP	17292X	29/12/1977	Mat Prov, PRAW, Suppl to BSAP R FO, 18th Sched, 11 December 1975, p.5
Nightingale, H. W.	PRO	16714R	08/05/1975	Mat Prov, PRAW, Suppl to BSAP R FO, 24th Sched, 29 December 1977, p.2
Nobes, Phillip Aubrey	PRO	17900F	29/12/1977	Mash Prov, PRAW, Suppl to BSAP R FO, 15th Sched, 8 May 1975, p.3
Norvall, W. P.	PRP	11399P	29/12/1977	Mash Prov, PRAW, Suppl to BSAP R FO, 24th Sched, 29 December 1977, p.2
Olds, Gordon Richard	PRO	4811D	29/12/1977	Mat Prov, PRAW, Suppl to BSAP R FO, 24th Sched, 29 December 1977, p.2
Page, M. V.	PRO	6879B	29/12/1977	Vic Prov, PRAW, Suppl to BSAP R FO, 24th Sched, 29 December 1977, p.4
Palmer, Philip Percy 'Phil'	PRP	7006P	29/12/1977	Mid Prov, PRAW, Suppl to BSAP R FO, 24th Sched, 29 December 1977, p.2
Parker, E.	PRP	8324X	08/05/1975	PGHQ, PRAW, Suppl to BSAP R FO, 24th Sched, 29 December 1977, p.3
Parker, L. G.	PRO	7626N	29/12/1977	Mid Prov, PRAW, Suppl to BSAP R FO, 15th Sched, 8 May 1975, p.8
Pascall, R. C.	PRO	17176T	11/12/1975	Mid Prov, PRAW, Suppl to BSAP R FO, 24th Sched, 29 December 1977, p.2
Pascoe, Ronald Geoffrey 'Ronnie'	PRP	6196J	23/08/1973	Man Prov, PRAW, Suppl to BSAP R FO, 18th Sched, 11 December 1975, p.3
Patterson, R. J.	PRP	21407S	29/12/1977	Mash Prov, PRAW, Suppl to BSAP R FO, 12th Sched, 23 August 1973, p.1
Paxton, D. H.	PRO	22014C	29/12/1977	PGHQ, PRAW, Suppl to BSAP R FO, 24th Sched, 29 December 1977, p.3
Perkins, William T. 'Bill'	PRO	8033F	11/12/1975	Mid Prov, PRAW, Suppl to BSAP R FO, 24th Sched, 29 December 1977, p.3
Plant, John Farmer	PRP	15333Q	29/05/1975	Man Prov, PRAW, Suppl to BSAP R FO, 18th Sched, 11 December 1975, p.1

Name	Rank	Number	Date	Award Source & Date (*continued*)
Plaskett, W. .E	PRP	17505B	29/12/1977	Sby Prov, PRAW, Suppl to BSAP R FO, 16th Sched, 29 May 1975, p.2
Potgieter, J. L.	PRP	16541D	29/12/1977	Mat Prov, PRAW, Suppl to BSAP R FO, 24th Sched, 29 December 1977, p.2
Pritchard, N. B.	PRO	13053M	29/12/1977	Mash Prov, PRAW, Suppl to BSAP R FO, 24th Sched, 29 December 1977, p.1
Purkis, C. S.	PRO	20308Y	29/12/1977	Mash Prov, PRAW, Suppl to BSAP R FO, 24th Sched, 29 December 1977, p.1
Quinn, J.	PRO	22015D	29/12/1977	Vic Prov, PRAW, Suppl to BSAP R FO, 24th Sched, 29 December 1977, p.4
Rawson, P. C.	PRP	9689F	08/05/1975	Mid Prov, PRAW, Suppl to BSAP R FO, 24th Sched, 29 December 1977, p.3
Reid, B. B. St J.	PRO	7846C	29/12/1977	Sby Prov, PRAW, Suppl to BSAP R FO, 15th Sched, 8 May 1975, p.10
Richards, Peter W.	PRP	22006T	29/12/1977	Mash Prov, PRAW, Suppl to BSAP R FO, 24th Sched, 29 December 1977, p.1
Roberts, L. F.	PRP	21908M	29/12/1977	Mash Prov, PRAW, Suppl to BSAP R FO, 24th Sched, 29 December 1977, p.2
Rogers, David	PRP	4062P	07/05/1970	Mat Prov, PRAW, Suppl to BSAP R FO, 24th Sched, 29 December 1977, p.2
Rogers, J. P.	PRP	22490V	29/12/1977	PRAW, Suppl to BSAP R FO, 5th Sched, 7 May 1970, p.1
Sainsbury, R. W.	PRP	21053H	29/12/1977	PGHQ, PRAW, Suppl to BSAP R FO, 24th Sched, 29 December 1977, p.3
Scales, Peter Frank	PRP	8909H	08/01/1970	Mash Prov, PRAW, Suppl to BSAP R FO, 24th Sched, 29 December 1977, p.2
Seward, B. Richard T.	PRO	6215E	01/06/1977	PRAW, Suppl to BSAP R FO, 1st Sched, 8 Jan 1970, p.1
Simpson, M. H.	PRP	19611Q	29/12/1977	Mash Prov, PRAW, Suppl to BSAP R FO, 20th Sched, undated, p.1
Simpson, R. L.	PRO	19382R	29/12/1977	Mat Prov, PRAW, Suppl to BSAP R FO, 24th Sched, 29 December 1977, p.2
Smith, A. N.	PRP	21611P	29/12/1977	Mat Prov, PRAW, Suppl to BSAP R FO, 24th Sched, 29 December 1977, p.2
Smith, H. S. C.	PRO	23968B	29/12/1977	Mat Prov, PRAW, Suppl to BSAP R FO, 24th Sched, 29 December 1977, p.2
Smith, R. P.	PRP	3520A	08/05/1975	Mat Prov, PRAW, Suppl to BSAP R FO, 24th Sched, 29 December 1977, p.2
Stam, Angelos George	PRP	11104T	08/05/1975	Mash Prov, PRAW, Suppl to BSAP R FO, 15th Sched, 8 May 1975, p.2
Stanning, Thomas Ripley	PRO	5685D	29/12/1977	Sby Prov, PRAW, Suppl to BSAP R FO, 15th Sched, 8 May 1975, p.11
Steed, J. F.	PRP	20787T	29/12/1977	Mash Prov, PRAW, Suppl to BSAP R FO, 24th Sched, 29 December 1977, p.1
Stockley, D. J.	PRO	22145V	29/12/1977	Mash Prov, PRAW, Suppl to BSAP R FO, 24th Sched, 29 December 1977, p.2
Strever, Edward Theodore	PRP	16034C	15/01/1970	Mid Prov, PRAW, Suppl to BSAP R FO, 24th Sched, 29 December 1977, p.3
Style, C. S.	PRP	8653E	29/12/1977	PRAW, Suppl to BSAP R FO, 2nd Sched, 15 Jan 1970, p.1
Tayler, J. R.	PRP	23356L	29/12/1977	Vic Prov, PRAW, Suppl to BSAP R FO, 24th Sched, 29 December 1977, p.4
Taylor, T. A.	PRO	20097T	29/12/1977	Vic Prov, PRAW, Suppl to BSAP R FO, 24th Sched, 29 December 1977, p.4
Thompson, A. S. C.	PRO	21882J	29/12/1977	Mat Prov, PRAW, Suppl to BSAP R FO, 24th Sched, 29 December 1977, p.2
Thorne, C. J.	PRP	24996T	20/12/1979	Mat Prov, PRAW, Suppl to BSAP R FO, 24th Sched, 29 December 1977, p.2
Thorne, P. B.	PRP	24827K	21/07/1979	Mash Prov, PRAW, Suppl to BSAP R FO, 59th Sched, undated, p.1
van Aardt, F.	PRO	18145X	11/12/1975	Sby Prov, PRAW, Suppl to BSAP R FO, 54th Sched, undated, p.4
van Buuren, Brian Anthony	PRP	9047H	29/12/1977	Man Prov, PRAW, Suppl to BSAP R FO, 18th Sched, 11 December 1975, p.3
van der Merwe, M. M.	PRO	17270W	29/12/1977	Man Prov, PRAW, Suppl to BSAP R FO, 24th Sched, 29 December 1977, p.1

Name	Rank	Number	Date	Award Source & Date (*continued*)
van der Riet, R. T.	PRP	19684V	29/12/1977	Mash Prov, PRAW, Suppl to BSAP R FO, 24th Sched, 29 December 1977, p.1
van Niekerk, A.	PRO	23940W	29/12/1977	Mat Prov, PRAW, Suppl to BSAP R FO, 24th Sched, 29 December 1977, p.2
Venter, David T. 'Dave'	PRO	20845G	01/06/1977	Mash Prov, PRAW, Suppl to BSAP R FO, 24th Sched, 29 December 1977, p.2
Vermaak, Johannes Martin	PRO	2624B	29/12/1977	Mash Prov, PRAW, Suppl to BSAP R FO, 20th Sched, undated, p.2
Walker, M. A.	PRO	23166E	29/12/1977	Vic Prov, PRAW, Suppl to BSAP R FO, 24th Sched, 29 December 1977, p.4
Waller, Noel Thornburg	PRP	12296P	29/12/1977	Mash Prov, PRAW, Suppl to BSAP R FO, 24th Sched, 29 December 1977, p.2
Walton, Peter P.	PRO	19214J	29/12/1977	Mash Prov, PRAW, Suppl to BSAP R FO, 24th Sched, 29 December 1977, p.1
Watson, J. R.	PRP	27065S	01/05/1981	Mash Prov, PRAW, Suppl to BSAP R FO, 24th Sched, 29 December 1977, p.2
Wesson, P. J. H.	PRP	7107Z	29/12/1977	Mat Prov, PRAW, Suppl to BSAP R FO, 65th Sched, undated, p.3
Willemse, J.	PRP	27618T	01/05/1981	Mat Prov, PRAW, Suppl to BSAP R FO, 24th Sched, 29 December 1977, p.2
Wilson, P. H. G.	PRP	22161M	29/12/1977	Man Prov, PRAW, Suppl to BSAP R FO, 66th Sched, May 1981, p.1
Winter, A. R.	PRO	16518D	29/12/1977	Mat Prov, PRAW, Suppl to BSAP R FO, 24th Sched, 29 December 1977, p.2
Wynne, I. L.	PRP	11581M	08/05/1975	Mat Prov, PRAW, Suppl to BSAP R FO, 24th Sched, 29 December 1977, p.2
York, G. H.	PRP	11552F	08/05/1975	Sby Prov, PRAW, Suppl to BSAP R FO, 15th Sched, 8 May 1975, p.11
Venter, David T. 'Dave'	PRO	20845G	01/06/1977	Sby Prov, PRAW, Suppl to BSAP R FO, 15th Sched, 8 May 1975, p.11
	Police Reserve Long Service Medal Police Reserve Air Wing			
Adams, J. P.	PRO	3812S	22/12/1971	RN 46/72, The Rhodesia Government Gazette, 14 January 1972, Vol.L, No.2, p.38
Addison, D. C.	PRP	14374Y	13/05/1980	GN 531/80, The Zimbabwe Government Gazette, 20 June 1980, Vol.LVIII, No.53, p.573
Aitken, J. W.	PRP	10097Z	20/01/1977	RN 202/77, The Rhodesia Government Gazette, 18 February 1977, Vol.LV, No.8, p.143
Anderson, R. L.	PRP	15099L	17/04/1981	GN 597/82, The Zimbabwean Government Gazette, 2 July 1982, Vol.LX, No.47, p.603
Anderson, S. M.	PRP	203886P	17/04/1981	GN 597/82, The Zimbabwean Government Gazette, 2 July 1982, Vol.LX, No.47, p.605
Anthony, M.	PRP	8806W	18/03/1977	RN 475/77, The Rhodesia Government Gazette, 22 April 1977, Vol.LV, No.20, p.362
Ashworth, M. G.	PRP	14188W	07/05/1979	RN 878/79, The Zimbabwe Rhodesia Government Gazette, 17 August 1979, Vol.LVII, No.49, p.711
Ball, J. S.	PRP	10395Y	30/08/1977	RN 1048/77, The Rhodesia Government Gazette, 30 September 1977, Vol.LV, No.49, p.866
Barton, W. H.	PRP	12274Q	02/11/1977	RN 1248/77, The Rhodesia Government Gazette, 25 November 1977, Vol.LV, No.59, p.1033
Bell, P. R.	PRO	3463N	28/06/1974	RN 1089/74, The Rhodesia Government Gazette, 26 July 1974, Vol.LII, No.40, p.870
Beniston, J. M.	PRO	15277E	17/04/1981	GN 597/82, The Zimbabwean Government Gazette, 2 July 1982, Vol.LX, No.47, p.602
Bickle, C. L.	PRP	12186V	02/11/1977	RN 1248/77, The Rhodesia Government Gazette, 25 November 1977, Vol.LV, No.59, p.1033
Boltt, C. R.	PRP	5791T	01/07/1971	RN 1152/71, The Rhodesia Government Gazette, 23 July 1971, Vol.XLIX, No.34, p,853
Bondi, I.	PRP	14228P	13/05/1980	GN 531/80, The Zimbabwe Government Gazette, 20 June 1980, Vol.LVIII, No.53, p.573
Bradshaw, F. J. S.	PRP	11114E	30/08/1977	RN 1048/77, The Rhodesia Government Gazette, 30 September 1977, Vol.LV, No.49, p.866
Brown, J. A.	PRP	14506R	13/05/1980	GN 531/80, The Zimbabwe Government Gazette, 20 June 1980, Vol.LVIII, No.53, p.573
Browne, V. A. D.	PRP	9022F	14/01/1975	RN 678/75, The Rhodesia Government Gazette, 9 May 1975, Vol.LIII, No.20, p.570

Name	Rank	Number	Date	Award Source & Date (*continued*)
Chisnall, H. V.	PRP	6110Q	22/12/1971	RN 46/72, The Rhodesia Government Gazette, 14 January 1972, Vol.L, No.2, p.37
Cowan, H.	PRP	11103S	20/01/1977	RN 202/77, The Rhodesia Government Gazette, 18 February 1977, Vol.LV, No.8, p.144
Crowley, K. L.	PRP	14574Q	13/05/1980	GN 531/80, The Zimbabwe Government Gazette, 20 June 1980, Vol.LVIII, No.53, p.573
Dawson, M. J.	PRP	7231J	02/11/1977	RN 1248/77, The Rhodesia Government Gazette, 25 November 1977, Vol.LV, No.59, p.1033
Dax, H. F.	PRP	4735W	22/12/1971	RN 46/72, The Rhodesia Government Gazette, 14 January 1972, Vol.L, No.2, p.37
de Jong, L. J.	PRO	13253E	07/05/1979	RN 878/79, The Zimbabwe Rhodesia Government Gazette, 17 August 1979, Vol.LVII, No.49, p.710
Dods-Brooks, S. H.	PRP	14918P	07/05/1980	GN 667/80, The Rhodesia Government Gazette, 1 August 1980, Vol.LVIII, No.62, p.710
Donnelly, F. J.	PRP	6828W	10/03/1973	RN 457/73, The Rhodesia Government Gazette, 30 March 1973, Vol.LI, No.16, p.316
Engles, L. T.	PRP	15709Z	17/04/1981	GN 597/82, The Zimbabwean Government Gazette, 2 July 1982, Vol.LX, No.47, p.604
Gibson, D. E.	PRO	7936A	14/01/1975	RN 183/75, The Rhodesia Government Gazette, 31 January 1975, Vol.LIII, No.5, p.120
Griffin, M. L.	PRP	9391G	02/11/1977	RN 1248/77, The Rhodesia Government Gazette, 25 November 1977, Vol.LV, No.59, p.1033
Grobler, P. S.	PRP	10587G	30/08/1977	RN 1048/77, The Rhodesia Government Gazette, 30 September 1977, Vol.LV, No.49, p.866
Haasbroek, C.F.	PRP	11473V	02/11/1977	RN 1248/77, The Rhodesia Government Gazette, 25 November 1977, Vol.LV, No.59, p.1033
Harvey, G. J. W.	PRP	20932B	17/04/1981	GN 597/82, The Zimbabwean Government Gazette, 2 July 1982, Vol.LX, No.47, p.603
Henderson, I. M.	PRP	8523N	14/01/1975	RN 678/75, The Rhodesia Government Gazette, 9 May 1975, Vol.LIII, No.20, p.570
Howell, D. L. M.	PRP	6558C	10/03/1973	RN 457/73, The Rhodesia Government Gazette, 30 March 1973, Vol.LI, No.16, p.316
Hurley, V.	PRP	14495E	13/05/1980	GN 531/80, The Zimbabwe Government Gazette, 20 June 1980, Vol.LVIII, No.53, p.573
Knight, O. H.	PRP	13747R	09/09/1979	RN 1075/79, The Zimbabwe Rhodesia Government Gazette, 19 October 1979, Vol.LVII, No.59, p.893
Linfield, G. W. R.	PRP	25829Z	17/04/1981	GN 597/82, The Zimbabwean Government Gazette, 2 July 1982, Vol.LX, No.47, p.602
Ludgater, W. J.	PRP	6282C	22/12/1971	RN 46/72, The Rhodesia Government Gazette, 14 January 1972, Vol.L, No.2, p.38
Lyon, D. H.	PRO	6477P	22/12/1971	RN 46/72, The Rhodesia Government Gazette, 14 January 1972, Vol.L, No.2, p.38
MacDonald, W. A. R.	PRP	5145R	01/07/1971	RN 1152/71, The Rhodesia Government Gazette, 23 July 1971, Vol.XLIX, No.34, p.854
Magee, J. H.	PRP	6998F	14/01/1975	RN 678/75, The Rhodesia Government Gazette, 9 May 1975, Vol.LIII, No.20, p.570
Manning, J. L.	PRP	6380J	10/03/1973	RN 457/73, The Rhodesia Government Gazette, 30 March 1973, Vol.LI, No.16, p.316
Norvall, W. P.	PRP	11399D	02/11/1977	RN 1248/77, The Rhodesia Government Gazette, 25 November 1977, Vol.LV, No.59, p.1033
Page, M. V.	PRO	6879B	10/03/1973	RN 457/73, The Rhodesia Government Gazette, 30 March 1973, Vol.LI, No.16, p.317
Palmer, P. P.	PRP	7006P	14/01/1975	RN 678/75, The Rhodesia Government Gazette, 9 May 1975, Vol.LIII, No.20, p.570
Palmer, P. P.	PRP	7006P	14/10/1975	RN 1497/75, The Rhodesia Government Gazette, 31 October 1975, Vol.LIII, No.49, p.1264
Parker, E.	PRP	8324X	28/06/1974	RN 1089/74, The Rhodesia Government Gazette, 26 July 1974, Vol.LII, No.40, p.870
Parker, L. G.	PRO	7626N	14/01/1975	RN 183/75, The Rhodesia Government Gazette, 31 January 1975, Vol.LIII, No.5, p.120
Pascoe, R. G.	PRP	6196J	22/12/1971	RN 46/72, The Rhodesia Government Gazette, 14 January 1972, Vol.L, No.2, p.38
Perkins, W. T.	PRO	8033F	14/01/1975	RN 183/75, The Rhodesia Government Gazette, 31 January 1975, Vol.LIII, No.5, p.120
Plant, J. F.	PRP	15333Q	17/04/1981	GN 597/82, The Zimbabwean Government Gazette, 2 July 1982, Vol.LX, No.47, p.604

Name	Rank	Number	Date	Award Source & Date *(continued)*
Prior, T. R.	PRO	11258L	02/11/1977	RN 1248/77, The Rhodesia Government Gazette, 25 November 1977, Vol.LV, No.59, p.1033
Scales, P. F.	PRP	8909H	14/01/1975	RN 678/75, The Rhodesia Government Gazette, 9 May 1975, Vol.LIII, No.20, p.570
Seward, B. R. T.	PRO	6215E	10/03/1973	RN 457/73, The Rhodesia Government Gazette, 30 March 1973, Vol.LI, No.16, p.316
Simon, E.	PRP	14520G	13/05/1980	GN 531/80, The Zimbabwe Government Gazette, 20 June 1980, Vol.LVIII, No.53, p.573
Smith, R. P.	PRP	3520A	18/03/1977	RN 475/77, The Rhodesia Government Gazette, 22 April 1977, Vol.LV, No.20, p.362
Stam, A. G.	PRP	11104T	20/01/1977	RN 202/77, The Rhodesia Government Gazette, 18 February 1977, Vol.LV, No.8, p.144
Stanning, T. R.	PRO	5685D	02/11/1977	RN 1248/77, The Rhodesia Government Gazette, 25 November 1977, Vol.LV, No.59, p.1033
Stevenson, C. G.	PRO	13158B	08/11/1977	RN 1260/77, The Rhodesia Government Gazette, 2 December 1977, Vol.LV, No.60, p.1051
Style, R. E.	PRP	8899X	14/01/1975	RN 678/75, The Rhodesia Government Gazette, 9 May 1975, Vol.LIII, No.20, p.570
van Jaarsveldt, A. B.	PRO	14943R	17/04/1981	GN 597/82, The Zimbabwean Government Gazette, 2 July 1982, Vol.LX, No.47, p.602
Vermaak, J. M.	PRO	2624B	03/12/1970	RN 72/71, The Rhodesia Government Gazette, 15 Jan 1971, Vol.XLIX, No.3, p.56
Waller, N. T.	PRP	12296P	15/06/1979	RN 752/79, The Zimbabwe Rhodesia Government Gazette, 6 July 1979, Vol.LVII, No. 41, p.592
York, G. H.	PRP	11552F	20/01/1977	RN 202/77, The Rhodesia Government Gazette, 18 February 1977, Vol.LV, No.8, p.144

VP-YJX is an Auster A.O.P.5 c/n 2051 ex-military TW507, then in November 1949 it was transferred to the civilian register as G-AKWH. It was exported to Kenya as VP-KID and then to Rhodesia in September 1952 as VP-YJX. It moved through six owners before Friedrich Wolf purchased the airframe and flew it regularly until 1971. When Wolf was refused entry to PRAW because of his age he handed the aircraft to his son-in-law, Peter Bell, who had been a PRAW observer since 1962, stipulating that it had to be used in PRAW.
Peter Bell Copper 115 was a member of the Mazoe Flight, and the aircraft was known to have been flown by several members of the Flight, including Hugh Chisnall pictured here. (Keith Chisnal)

Appendix IV

PRAW Hire Rates 1 June 1979

Type of Aircraft	Private Rate	Commercial Rate
Auster	$31.50	$34.50
Cessna 172	$32.50	$35.50
Cessna 175	$39.25	$42.25
Cessna 177	$39.75	$42.75
Cessna 172 Reims	$39.75	$42.75
Cherokee 140		$32.40
Cherokee 180	$35.75	$38.75
Cherokee Arrow 180	$40.25	$43.25
Cherokee Arrow 200	$41.75	$44.75
Partenavia	$38.75	$41.75
Mooney	$45.50	$48.50
Beech Sundowner	$36.75	$39.75
Beech Bonanza	$52.25	$54.25
Cessna 180	$48.75	$51.75
Cessna 182	$49.25	$52.25
Cessna 185	$53.75	$56.75
Cessna 185 (Float)	$67.75	$70.75
Cessna 206	$56.50	$59.50
Cessna 206 (Turbo)	$59.00	$62.00
Cessna 207	$62.50	$65.50
Cessna 210	$60.50	$63.50

Cessna 210 (Turbo)	$63.50	$66.50
Cherokee 235	$47.00	$50.00
Cherokee 6/260	$52.75	$55.75
Cherokee 6/300	$56.00	$59.00
Comanche 250	$50.25	$53.25
Aztec	$90.50	$95.00
Cessna 310	$92.00	$96.50
Cessna 337	$70.75	$75.25

Bibliography

Publications

Baker, C. *Revolt of the Ministers: The Malawi Cabinet Crisis 1964–1965*, (London: I. B. Tauris, 2001 Illustrated edition)

Barker, Jim, *Zimbabwe Paradise Plundered*, (Alberton, South Africa: Galago Publishing Pty 2013)

Binda, A. Masjoda, *The History of the Rhodesian African Rifles*, (Johannesburg, South Africa: 30 Degrees South Publishers 2007)

Brent, Winston, *Rhodesian Air Force – The Sanctions Busters*, (Ottowa, Canada: Freeworld Publications 2001)

Collier, E. B. 'Rhodesia's Police Reserve Air Wing' in *The Police Journal: Theory, Practice and Principles* September 1965, (London: Sage Publications 2005)

Cole, Barbara, *The Elite, The Story of the Rhodesian Special Air Services* (Pietermaritzburg, South Africa: Three Knights Publishing, 1984)

Elliott, B., 'Police Aviation A History Part Two,' in *Police Aviation News* (Waltham Abbey: Police Aviation Research, 1934) Frame, John, *The Rhodesian Civil War (1966–1979)* (London: New Generation Publishing, 2018) Kennerley, W. 'Flying Coppers,' in *Medal News*, February 2008 (Exeter: Token Publishing, 2008) Kennerley, W. 'Rhodesia's Second Air Force, The Story of the British South Africa Police Reserve Air Wing, Part II of From Horse to Aeroplane' (Harlow: BSAP Regimental Association, 2015)

Petter-Bowyer, P. J. H. *Winds of Destruction* (Bloomington, Indiana: Trafford Publishing 2003)

PA-28-235 Cherokee VP-YYE of Securitas in the Mount Hampden Hangars in 1971/72. It was noted on the BSAP Nominal Roll of Aircraft in 1974. (Robin D. W. Norton)

Owned by Copper 13 Sarel Haasbroek Piper PA-28-180 Cherokee C VP-YYF is on the hard standing at Charles Prince Airport. The person walking passed the aircraft is reportedly Tony Oats Copper 33 of the Lomagundi Flight. (Robin D. W. Norton)

John Plant's Techair company owned and operated Piper PA-28-180C Cherokee and it is known that Mike Gardener flew this on PRAW duties. (Robin D. W. Norton)

Russell, N., Phillips, H., Hamley, R., Gibbs, P. *Blue and Old Gold: The History of the British South Africa Police 1889–1980,* vol. III (Johannesburg, South Africa: 30 Degrees South Publishers, 2009)

Skipworth-Michell, Noick, *Operation Enterprise: The Battle for Salisbury, Rhodesia* (Toronto, Canada: Rakuten Kobo, 2020)

Steed, J., *Cowboys Don't Fly* (London: Reach Publishers, 2019)

Salt, B., *A Pride of Eagles: The Definitive History of the Rhodesian Air Force, 1920–1980,* (Johannesburg, South Africa: Covos Day, 2001)

Wood, J. R. T., *A Matter of Weeks Rather Than Months: The Impasse Between Harold Wilson and Ian Smith Sanctions, Aborted Settlements and War 1965–1969* (Bloomington, Indiana: Trafford Publishing, 2012)

Wood, J. R. T., *The War Diaries of André Dennison* (Gibraltar: Ashanti Publishing, 1989)

Unpublished Works

Cawood, P. *303 British South Africa Police – A Young Woman's Call Sign during the Rhodesian War*. Unpublished ms.

Jeater, D. and Onslow, S. and Berry, A. (2013) Rhodesian forces oral history project.

Onslow, Professor Sue, 'Why Did You Fight?' Narratives of the Rhodesian War c.1970–1980', papers deposited in University of the West of England, 2006–2008

Websites

B.S.A.P. Regimental Association, The Magazines & Regimental Records of the B.S.A.P., Digital Library

Chadya, Joyce (interviewer), & Kanhinge, Esther (interviewee). (2003). *Interview with Esther Kanhinge* [Interviews]. Private Collection.

https://jstor.org/stable/al.sff.document.chadya0001

http://www.jrtwood.com/article_fireforce.asp

https://rhodesianheritage.blogspot.com/2014/03/operation-enterprise-battle-for.html

University of the West of England, http://researchdata.uwe.ac.uk/104.

NOTES

Chapter 1

1 Quotes from T Mann from personal e-mail correspondence.

2 M Norton, https://rhodesianheritage.blogspot.com/2014/03/operation-enterprise-battle-for.html

3 T Mann, personal e-mail correspondence.

4 *1890 Mashonaland Medal, 1893 Matabeleland Medal, 1896 Rhodesia Medal and 1897 Mashonaland Medal,* (Berkshire, Roberts Publications), p.1.

Chapter 2

1 Alan Abrey personal email to Wayne Kennerley.

2 Tony Mann personal email to Guy Ellis.

3 Old Rhodesian Air Force Sods https://orafs1.rssing.com/

4 Mark Brightman mail to ORAFS

5 *Natal Outpost* editions 93 and 94.

Chapter 3

1 First published in *the Natal Outpost* No 93, October 2013 and No 94, May 2014. Reprinted with the permission of the BASP Association KwaZulu Natal. And with the kind permission of his daughter Gill Brown. Also in ORAFs 15 October 2012.

2 Author Gerry Cleveland, republished with permission.

3 John Munro via email to Guy Ellis.

4 Written by Bob Needham and published with permission.

5 Note: The 'Roll of Honour' in *Masodja, The History of The Rhodesian African Rifles*, Aleandre Binda, records this soldier's name as Private Julious Tarusari of 2nd Battalion Rhodesian African Rifles, no company is recorded.

6 Written by John Tayler via email to Guy Ellis.

About the Author

In the late 1980s, Guy Ellis began writing aviation articles as a volunteer at the Cape Town Branch of the SAAF Museum. Initially, he contributed to the newsletter, and later took on the role of Editor and contributor for *Air Heritage*, the museum's annual magazine. Through this period, he successfully completed a degree in History and Ancient History, as well as a Masters in Management Engineering, while employed fulltime in the IT industry.

He has authored numerous articles for aviation and naval magazines and e-publications. Additionally, he has built and managed the website for a prominent UK aviation museum, while also maintaining his personal website at www.historyjournal.co.uk.

His published works include notable titles such as *Serve to Save: The South African Air Force at Sea*, *Gloucestershire Airport Through Time*, *Britain's Jet Age 1&2*, and WK275: *The Restoration and Preservation of the Last Supermarine Swift F4.*

Currently living in rural Gloucestershire, he continues to explore little known stories from history, preserving and documenting these for this and future generations, making significant contributions to the field, showcasing his passion for preserving and documenting the rich heritage of aviation.